Writers at Work

The Essay

Dorothy E. Zemach
Lynn Stafford-Yilmaz

CAMBRIDGE UNIVERSITY PRESS
Cambridge, New York, Melbourne, Madrid, Cape Town,
Singapore, São Paulo, Delhi, Mexico City

Cambridge University Press
32 Avenue of the Americas, New York, NY 10013-2473, USA

www.cambridge.org
Information on this title: www.cambridge.org/9780521693028

First published 2008
8th printing 2012

Printed in the United States of America

A catalog record for this book is available from the British Library.

Library of Congress Cataloging-in-Publication Data
Zemach, Dorothy E.
Writers at work. the essay / Dorothy E. Zemach, Lynn Stafford-Yilmaz.
          p. cm.
ISBN 978-0-521-69302-8
          1. English language—Textbooks for foreign speakers. 2. English
language—Rhetoric—Problems, exercises, etc. 3. Report writing—
Problems, exercises, etc. I. Stafford-Yilmaz, Lynn. II. Title.
III. Title: Essay.

PE1128.Z46 2008
428.2'4—dc22   2007040730

ISBN 978-0-521-69302-8 student's book
ISBN 978-0-521-69303-5 teacher's manual

Cambridge University Press has no responsibility for the persistence or accuracy of
urls for external or third-party Internet Web sites referred to in this book, and does
not guarantee that any content on such Web sites is, or will remain, accurate or
appropriate.

Art direction and book design: Adventure House, NYC
Layout services: TSI Graphics
Illustration credits: Carlos Castellanos, pages 6, 11, 17, 19, 21, 29, 32, 46, 54, 56, 60,
75, 102, 103, 104, 153

Table of Contents

Chapter Contents

Essay Writing Basics

CHAPTER 1 Explanatory Essays

* The items in this column refer to the titles of the
information boxes that appear throughout the book.

CHAPTER 2 Problem-Solution Essays

CHAPTER 3 Comparison-Contrast Essays

CHAPTER 4 Persuasive Essays

CHAPTER 5 Responding to a Reading

CHAPTER 6   Timed Essays

Introduction

THE *WRITERS AT WORK* SERIES

The *Writers at Work* series takes beginning to high intermediate-level writing students through a process approach to writing. The series is intended primarily for adults whose first language is not English, but it may also prove effective for younger writers or for native speakers of English who are developing their competence as independent writers in English.

- *Writers at Work: From Sentence to Paragraph* prepares beginning to high beginning students to write grammatically accurate, topic-related sentences as the basis for an introduction to paragraph writing.

- *Writers at Work: The Paragraph* prepares high beginning to low intermediate students to write well-developed paragraphs using a variety of organization types.

- *Writers at Work: The Short Composition* prepares low intermediate to intermediate-level students to put together several paragraphs to write well-constructed and well-edited short compositions.

- *Writers at Work: The Essay* prepares intermediate to high intermediate students to write fully-developed essays with an introduction, body paragraphs, and a conclusion. Upon completion of this book, students will be ready for more advanced-level academic writing courses.

The approach

Competence in writing comes from knowing *how* to write as much as from knowing *what* to write. That is why the *Writers at Work* books are organized around the process of writing. They teach students about the writing process and then guide them to use it as they write. We believe that once students understand how to use the writing process in writing sentences, paragraphs, short compositions, and essays, they will gain the confidence they need to advance to more complex writing tasks.

In teaching writing to lower-level students, there is always the danger of sacrificing creativity in order to achieve accuracy, or vice versa. The *Writers at Work* books guide students through the writing process in such a way that their final pieces of writing are not only expressive and rich in content, but also clear and accurate.

ABOUT *WRITERS AT WORK: THE ESSAY*

Chapter structure

Each chapter is divided into the following five parts:

I Getting Started

Students are stimulated to think about the topic of the chapter. They read and analyze a sample essay, select a topic for their own writing, and begin the process of generating ideas.

II Preparing the First Draft

Students organize, plan, and write their first draft. They study language structures that are likely to occur in the type of essay featured in the chapter.

III Revising Your Writing

Students analyze specific parts of an essay, practice new writing skills, and apply what they learn to the revision of their first draft. Working in pairs, students offer each other feedback before they revise.

IV Editing Your Writing

Students are introduced to selected aspects of grammar and mechanics. They edit their writing for accurate grammar and for more sophisticated ways to use vocabulary and structure before producing their final draft.

V Following Up

Students share their writing with one another. Finally, they fill out a self-assessment form, which allows them to track their progress as writers throughout the course.

Key features

- The book begins with an introductory section, "Essay Writing Basics," which reviews the basic elements of an essay, including format, thesis statements, topic sentences, main ideas and supporting details, conclusions, and titles. This section lays the foundation for the chapters that follow.

- The six chapters of the book present common organizational patterns and types of writing used in formal essay writing. All of the activities and exercises in a chapter relate to the pattern or type of writing. In this way, students are able to apply what they learn in their own writing.

- The final chapter prepares students to write timed essays such as they might encounter in classroom situations, in writing examinations, or when they apply to college or graduate school.

- The book uses examples of student writing, including complete sample essays, sample paragraphs, and isolated sentences. These have been chosen for their representative nature and their engaging content. The activities in the book guide students through analysis, revision, and editing of these writing samples as models for their own writing.

- The book encourages students to make the connection between thinking and writing. It structures activities that force students to think logically and openly as they focus their writing. The activities enable students to explore the relationship between ideas and the effort of expressing them.

- Collaborating tasks and peer feedback activities in the text make learning to write an enjoyable and stimulating activity. Through interaction with other readers and their ideas, writers see the impact of their writing and the interplay of writers' and readers' thoughts.

Acknowledgements

We would like to thank our students and colleagues, whose individual talents and collective hard work have enriched *Writers at Work: The Essay* beyond anything we could have done alone.

First, we would like to thank our students at the many schools and language centers where we have taught over the past many years. Their writing, trials, questions, and growth as writers, have provided the framework for the presentation of our ideas in this text.

We would like to thank a handful of students in particular, for stepping outside of the call of duty to share their writing for publication in this book. These include Sunsanee Anuchitpailin, Miguel A. Caban Ruiz, Melissa Carrasco, Fred Kalema, Stacy Lee, Kodjo Maku, Yuki Nagami, Gabriela Richards, Miwa Sakai, Ann Santitanon, and Victor Yang.

In addition to these students, our colleagues have offered us generous support, professional insight, and friendly advice. Special thanks to Amy Fenning, Kwansei Gakuin University School of Policy Studies ELP (Japan); Professor Leonardo Flores and Cathy Mazak, University of Puerto Rico at Mayagüez; Timothy Healy, American Cultural Exchange at Seattle Pacific University; Mark Paulson, Bellevue Community College; Susan Rankin, University of Oregon; Garnet Templin-Imel, Bellevue Community College; Julie Vorholt, San Jose State University; and Bill Walker, University of Oregon.

We would like to thank the following reviewers for their insights: Judith Garcia, Miami Dade College; Tim McDaniel, Green River Community College; Jennifer Summerhays, Passaic County Community College; Evelyn E. Uyemura, El Camino Community College; and Jack Miller, Normandale Community College. Timothy Healy also provided invaluable feedback after piloting several chapters of this book with his students.

Thank you also to Adam L. Penenberg for sharing his work and allowing its adaptation.

At Cambridge University Press, we owe our highest thanks to Bernard Seal, commissioning editor, who dove into the revising ring with his sleeves rolled up, reminding us once again that the writing process truly is a process. Thanks also to the project editor, Sylvia Dare; in-house development editor, Ann Pascoe-van Zyl; and to the copyeditor, Linda LiDestri.

Finally, thanks to Jennifer Bixby, our development editor, who worked with care and professionalism, forcing us to look beyond our original scope and to harvest the core of each idea that we have aimed to present in this book.

Essay Writing Basics

In this section, you will learn what an essay is and what the basic steps involved in writing an essay are. You will see that a good essay has a strong topic, a specific purpose, and that it is written for a specific audience. You will learn that writing is a process that requires planning, revision, and time.

I WHAT IS AN ESSAY?

A Define an essay

Work with a partner to take this quiz about essays and writing. Circle the best answers. Then discuss your answers with your classmates.

1 The definition of the word *essay* is ____.
   a a long paragraph on a single topic
   b a piece of writing that is long enough to cover many topics and present different viewpoints
   c a piece of writing on a single subject, usually presenting the personal view of the writer

2 An essay is a type of writing that you normally do ____.
   a in a work situation
   b at the high school or college level
   c when you want to tell a story

3 When writing an essay, it is ____ acceptable to write in the first person (using *I* and *me*).
   a almost always
   b sometimes
   c never

4 It's a good idea to write ____ of an essay.
   a just one draft
   b several drafts
   c at least eight drafts

5 A *topic* is ____.
   a a specific subject; what the essay is about
   b an opinion; what you think
   c a broad field; all of your ideas in a given area

6 A *topic sentence* is a sentence that ____.
   a is the first one in a paragraph
   b is the most interesting
   c tells what the paragraph is about

7 In an essay, the *introduction* ____.
   a introduces the writer
   b introduces the topic and your opinion about it
   c introduces the reason you chose your topic

8 The *thesis statement*, or main idea, of an essay appears in the ____.
   a title
   b introduction
   c body (middle paragraphs)

9 The *conclusion* of an essay often _____.
   a restates the thesis
   b is not indented
   c presents details about a new topic

10 Most of the *examples* and *support* in an essay appear in _____ .
   a the introduction
   b the body paragraphs
   c the conclusion

11 Most essays in high school and college are about _____ long.
   a three paragraphs
   b five to ten paragraphs
   c five to ten pages

12 When you write an academic essay, your *audience* is usually _____.
   a yourself
   b your friends and family
   c your teacher and classmates

B Notice essay format

ESSAY FORMAT

Essays follow a certain format; that is, they are written in a standard style that is easy to read. Your teacher may give you specific instructions for the essays you write in your class, but here are some general guidelines.

- **Required information:** Follow your instructor's directions for information to include at the top of your essay, such as your name, the class name, date, and so on.
- **Title:** Your title should be centered. Do not capitalize every letter of the title. Capitalize only the first letter of major words (nouns, pronouns, verbs, adjectives, and adverbs). Capitalize only short words like *the* and *a* if they are the first word in the title.
- **Spacing:** Use double-spacing on a computer or, if handwriting, write on every other line. This way, your instructor can easily write comments on your essay.
- **Indentation:** Indent the first sentence of every paragraph by leaving a space about $\frac{1}{2}$ an inch wide (about 1.25 cm). On a computer, this length is usually preset as five spaces with the tab key.
- **Margins:** Leave margins of about 1 inch or 2.55 cm on the left, right, top, and bottom of your essay. On a computer, margins are preset.
- **Fonts:** If you use a computer, use 12-point regular (not bold or italic) style font. Don't use unusual fonts or more than one font.
- **Alignment:** Format your essay *flush left:* The left side of each line starts at the same place (except for the indented first line of new paragraphs). Lines on the right side should be *ragged* – that is, they do not have to end at the same place.

Practice 1

Read the model essay below. Label the parts with letters from the box. The number in parentheses shows a term that is used three times.

a body paragraph (3)	**e** indent	**i** right margin	**m** top margin
b bottom margin	**f** introduction	**j** support	**n** topic sentence (3)
c conclusion	**g** left margin	**k** thesis statement	
d example	**h** required information	**l** title	

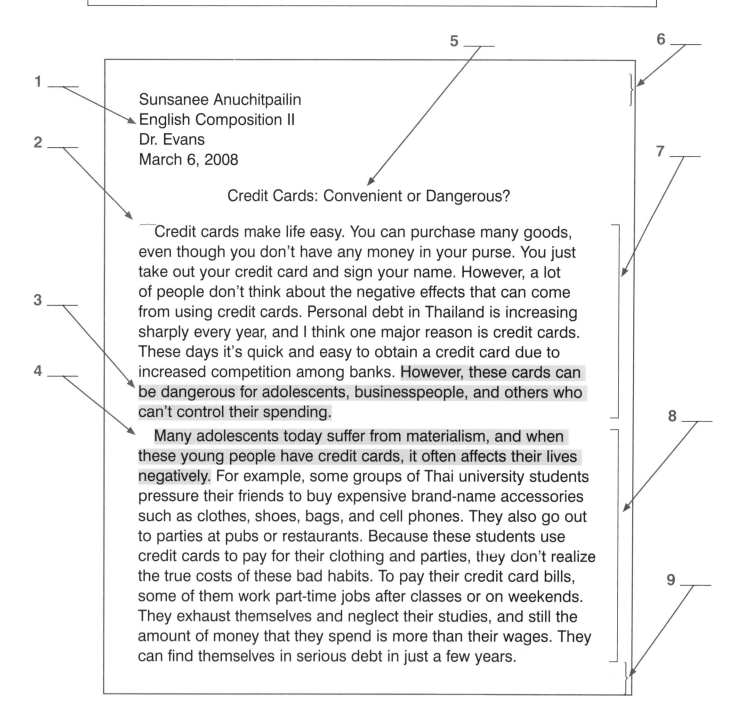

5 _____ 6 _____

1 _____

Sunsanee Anuchitpailin
English Composition II
Dr. Evans
March 6, 2008

2 _____

7 _____

Credit Cards: Convenient or Dangerous?

Credit cards make life easy. You can purchase many goods, even though you don't have any money in your purse. You just take out your credit card and sign your name. However, a lot of people don't think about the negative effects that can come from using credit cards. Personal debt in Thailand is increasing sharply every year, and I think one major reason is credit cards. These days it's quick and easy to obtain a credit card due to increased competition among banks. However, these cards can be dangerous for adolescents, businesspeople, and others who can't control their spending.

3 _____

4 _____

8 _____

Many adolescents today suffer from materialism, and when these young people have credit cards, it often affects their lives negatively. For example, some groups of Thai university students pressure their friends to buy expensive brand-name accessories such as clothes, shoes, bags, and cell phones. They also go out to parties at pubs or restaurants. Because these students use credit cards to pay for their clothing and parties, they don't realize the true costs of these bad habits. To pay their credit card bills, some of them work part-time jobs after classes or on weekends. They exhaust themselves and neglect their studies, and still the amount of money that they spend is more than their wages. They can find themselves in serious debt in just a few years.

9 _____

If students have troubles with their debts, their parents may be able to help them. However, businesspeople who have trouble with debt face the risk of ruining their financial reputations. For example, they may end up on a blacklist, which is a record kept by financial companies. A blacklist shows if a person has had credit troubles. Banks will not approve a loan for a person who is on a blacklist, so that person won't be able to borrow money to run a business or to buy real estate. In addition, employees can also get into trouble at work if they have credit problems. For example, one of my co-workers owed money to his credit card company. Accordingly, the company phoned him at the office every day. He refused to receive his calls and told me to inform the creditor that he was in a meeting. After that, he asked to borrow some money from friends, but nobody trusted him. Fortunately, he later got a new job that earned him enough money to solve his credit problems. I am sure, though, that there are other businesspeople who were not as fortunate as my friend.

Credit card problems affect not only adolescents and businesspeople, but also average people who can't control their spending. Advertising leads people to believe that they need fancier products and more of them. If they just used cash, they would not be able to buy products they couldn't afford. However, credit cards allow them to spend money they don't really have. Then when they can't pay their monthly credit card bills, they must pay fees as well as high rates of interest on the money they still owe. In some cases, the interest rates can be 20 percent per month. Paying off their debt makes people poorer, which actually encourages them to use their credit cards more. This growing cycle of debt causes all kinds of social problems.

Credit cards can bring you convenience if you can manage your money and control your spending. But using credit cards will affect you in negative ways if you buy everything that you desire. They can lead you to debt, hurt your ability to do business, and damage your social stability. For these reasons, I believe that people should be better educated and also counseled about the risks when they apply for a credit card.

C Understand the purpose

PURPOSES FOR ESSAYS

The word *essay* comes from a French word meaning "to attempt," or "to try." Writing instructors therefore ask students to write essays that make a point and are written with a specific purpose in mind. The most common essay purposes are to:

- explain or discuss a topic and give a personal opinion
- identify a problem and its causes, and propose a solution
- compare and contrast two or more things
- persuade a reader to hold a certain opinion or take a certain action
- respond to a reading or lecture
- demonstrate understanding or writing skills by writing a timed essay in class

Although a writer may have several purposes, essays ultimately aim to persuade their readers. For example, by comparing and contrasting two things, the writer hopes to persuade readers of the superiority of one over the other.

For most essays written in high school or college, you will be required to express your personal opinion and include arguments to support it. Stating your opinion is important even when your essay includes factual information or focuses on another author's point of view.

Make sure that you understand the purpose of your essay before you begin to write it! Always ask your instructor if you are not certain.

Practice 2

Read the writer's idea for an essay. What is the purpose of the essay? Circle the letter of the purpose.

1 Korean and Chinese people have some similar physical features, but others that are often different. I want people to know the differences so they understand that we don't look the same.
   a to persuade the reader
   b to compare and contrast
   c to respond to information from a reading

2 I play the drums. Some of my friends think that I chose an easy instrument. I want people to know about playing drums so they understand why drumming is just as challenging as playing any other instrument.
   a to explain or discuss a topic
   b to demonstrate understanding or writing skill by writing a timed essay
   c to identify a problem and offer a solution

3 In my school, all articles in the student newspaper must be approved by the school administration before publication. I think this shows that the school doesn't respect students. Students should have complete freedom to express themselves in the student newspaper.
   a to identify a problem and offer a solution
   b to respond to infomation from a lecture
   c to compare and contrast

4 I read an article about different events leading up to the women's rights movement in my country. I want to summarize those causes and identify the major ones.
   a to compare and contrast
   b to identify a problem and offer a solution
   c to respond to information from a reading, lecture, or other source

5 *Prompt:* Think of an issue that you and your parents disagree about. Take 30 minutes to explain your different positions. *Writer's idea:* My parents consider "study" time to be time that I am sitting at a desk with my head in a book. However, there are other ways to study that are better for me.
   a to respond to information from a lecture
   b to explain or discuss a topic
   c to demonstrate understanding or writing skill by writing a timed essay

6 High school sports teams are too competitive. Only the good athletes can participate. School should have non-competitive sports teams, for health and fun. Teams should get points for attitude and effort, rather than goals or baskets.
   a to explain or discuss a topic
   b to persuade the reader
   c to compare or contrast

A Identify your audience

AUDIENCE

When you write an essay, someone is going to read it: your audience. Naturally, your instructor is one part of your audience. If your classmates will read your paper, they are also your audience. In addition, your instructor might ask you to imagine another audience; for example, a government official, the readers of your school newspaper, or the readers of a certain magazine.

When you write your essay, identify your audience. Think about what they might already know about your topic.

* Do they need any background information?
* Do they know a lot or a little about your topic?
* Do they have opinions about your topic? If so, are those opinions likely to be the same as or different from your own?

After you consider your audience's knowledge and beliefs about your topic, then you can choose the information and arguments that are most likely to interest and persuade your reader.

Practice 3

Imagine you are writing a paper to convince readers to change to a vegetarian diet. In the box are some elements you could include in your paper. Discuss the questions on the next page with a partner or in a group.

> **a** a brief definition of *vegetarianism*
>
> **b** a detailed definition of *vegetarianism*
>
> **c** arguments about how raising meat is harmful to the environment
>
> **d** arguments to show that eating meat is not good for your health
>
> **e** arguments to show that being vegetarian is less expensive than eating meat
>
> **f** arguments to show that changing to a vegetarian diet is easy
>
> **g** descriptions of vegetarian diets in other countries
>
> **h** examples of famous vegetarian people
>
> **i** explanation of how vegetarian diets can be introduced into schools
>
> **j** explanations of the health benefits of a vegetarian diet

1 Which elements from the box would you include for these different audiences? Which would you not include? Why?
- People who have no knowledge about vegetarianism
- People who are concerned about the environment and health
- People who are interested in world cultures
- People who don't have much time for cooking or money for food

2 Which audiences would be easiest to write for? Which would be the hardest?

Practice 4

Reread the essay "Credit Cards: Convenient or Dangerous?" on page 4 - 5. As you read, ask yourself, "What kind of reader did the writer imagine would read this essay?" In other words, who is the audience for the essay? Then answer the questions below. Discuss your answers with a partner. You don't have to agree on your answers, but be sure to explain your ideas.

1 Who is the intended audience for the essay?
  a only students
  b only business people
  c both students and working people

2 Before reading the article, what do many readers probably think about credit cards?
  a They are convenient.
  b They are dangerous.
  c They have mixed benefits and drawbacks.

3 What does the reader know about the problems the writer discusses?
  a a little; does not know about words like *blacklist*
  b some; might understand the problems with only a little explanation, but has not thought about them before
  c a lot; is looking only for details and new solutions to a very familiar problem

4 Why did the writer choose this topic?
  a She wanted to warn people about a problem and suggest a solution.
  b She wanted to criticize some kinds of people for being irresponsible.
  c She wanted to complain about the use of credit cards in Thailand.

5 What does the writer hope the reader will do or think after reading?
  a stop using credit cards
  b be careful when using credit cards
  c change some laws about credit card use

B Choose a topic

> **TOPIC SELECTION**
>
> The topic of an essay is often assigned. Your instructor may assign you a specific topic; but more often you will be assigned a more general topic or type of essay, and you will be free to choose the specific topic.
>
> There are several criteria for selecting a good topic, but one key is that you choose something that is interesting to you. If you like your own topic, you will have more energy and interest in writing about it. When you choose a topic that interests you, you will probably write a better essay.

Practice 5

Work with a partner. Read through the list of general topics below. Then make a quick list of two or three more focused topics for each. Compare your topics with another pair. Finally, from among your topics and those of the other two classmates, choose the one topic that interests you and your partner the most.

1 Take a position on education in your country.

   university entrance exams in my country

   the value and cost of "cram schools"

   the importance of getting into a good high school

2 Identify a threat to the environment *or* propose a solution.

   _____

   _____

   _____

3 Argue for or against using a certain type of technology.

   _____

   _____

   _____

4 Explain a useful piece of advice you received.

   _____

   _____

   _____

5 Describe a holiday in your country.

   _____

   _____

   _____

THE WRITING PROCESS

Writing, like many artistic endeavors, is a process; that is, the writer goes through different steps to create a final product. Beginning writers are sometimes surprised to learn how much work is done before they even start writing – as well as how much work is done after they write a first draft!

Beginning writers are also sometimes surprised to learn that writing is not always a linear process. Some steps may be repeated several times. In the end, a talented writer must pick and choose from the best parts, moving slowly toward a polished final product.

Practice 6

Below are the steps a painter takes to create a painting. Number the steps in order from 1 to 7. Write the number in the box in each picture.

She shows the painting to her friend. He gives his opinion and makes some suggestions.

She paints the painting.

She displays her painting.

She makes some changes based on his comments.

She generates ideas for her painting by making some rough sketches.

She chooses the parts of her sketches she likes best and organizes them.

The artist gets ideas from her own life and from seeing other people's paintings.

Practice 7

Below are the steps a writer goes through. Match them to the steps the painter uses in *Practice 6*, and write numbers on the lines.

_____ **a** writes the first draft

_____ **b** hands in her final paper for others to read and enjoy

_____ **c** organizes notes from brainstorming

_____ **d** brainstorms ideas onto paper

_____ **e** chooses a topic from reading, talking to other people, listening to lectures, personal experience, and so on

_____ **f** makes some changes and writes a second draft

_____ **g** gets feedback (comments) from a reader

Practice 8

Write a paragraph about the writing process. Use the information in *Practice 7* to help you. You can add information and details. Use the topic sentence below.

A writer goes through several steps to create an essay. First, ...

LEARNING FROM WRITING

For many writers, the process of writing is more than just putting ideas to paper. Instead, the act of writing inspires the writer to think differently and to think more carefully about the topic than before. The writer begins to understand the topic in a new way. In other words, the process of writing can focus and deepen the writer's understanding, or even change the writer's beliefs about the topic. This is, of course, one major reason students are assigned essays to write!

The process of learning while you write can be very exciting, as if new windows are opening up in your mind. At the same time, the process of learning while you write can be frustrating. Just when you think you've argued your point clearly, it may turn out that you yourself don't believe that point anymore.

A good writer is open to the possibility of learning while he or she writes, and understands that rewriting may be necessary to reflect that learning.

Explanatory Essays

Some people that we meet and some events in our lives have an important effect on us. What people and events have influenced or changed you?

In this chapter, you will write an essay that explains how a person or an event has changed your life. As you write your essay, you will follow every step of the writing process. You will learn about thesis statements and how to structure your essay with an effective introduction and conclusion.

A Think about the sample essay topic

You are going to read an essay by a student who explains how her school influenced the person that she is today. Before you read the essay, look at the information in the charts and discuss the questions that follow.

Figure 1.1 U.S. schools and grades

Age	Grades	School
3-4	Pre-K	Pre-kindergarten or preschool
5	K	Kindergarten
6-10	1-5	Elementary (primary) school
11-13	6-8	Middle school
14-18	9-12	High school (secondary school)
18-21	Freshman- first year Sophomore- second year Junior- third year Senior- fourth year	College or university (post-secondary or undergraduate education)
22+		Graduate school

Figure 1.2 Where U.S. students go to school

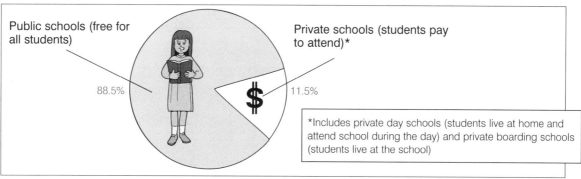

Public schools (free for all students) 88.5%

Private schools (students pay to attend)* 11.5%

*Includes private day schools (students live at home and attend school during the day) and private boarding schools (students live at the school)

Source: U.S. Department of Education

1 What types of schools have you attended?
2 How popular are private schools in the United States (see Figure 1.2) compared to those in another country you know about?
3 What are some differences between public and private schools? What do you think are some advantages and disadvantages of each type of school?
4 What grade or year in school was the most memorable for you? Which teacher was most memorable? Why?
5 Explain how your school experience helped prepare you for life.

B Read the sample essay

As you read the essay, ask yourself what the writer's main point is and whether the writer has explained clearly how her experience changed her. Then share your ideas with a partner.

Life Lessons from School

I hated school! Now, however, when I feel discouraged by my problems, I overcome this by trying to remember my years at boarding school. Those years were challenging and full of problems, but still, I gained a lot from them. After I graduated from elementary school, I left my family and went to live at a boarding school because my hometown was very far from my middle school. I stayed there until I graduated from high school. It was very difficult for me at first, but eventually I learned how to make true friends, obey rules, and return my parents' love. Even though these things were not easy to learn, the lessons from my boarding school experience made me an independent woman and a productive member of society.

Getting along with the other students and making friends was the first big challenge of boarding school. There were many different kinds of people at my school. I had six or seven roommates of different ages – from 12 years old to 18. They all had different hobbies and habits. Getting along with so many girls required a lot of patience and thoughtfulness. Therefore, at first we used to have quarrels. However, we had to face one another every day, so we tried to understand each other. Soon we realized that we had many of the same problems, such as being homesick, disliking certain classes, and feeling rebellious. We learned to find each other's good points. Slowly, my roommates became like sisters to me. Even now, the friends I made there are my treasures.

As a new student, I was famous because I did not like to obey the rules of the school. I wasn't used to following a lot of rules because when I had lived at home, my parents usually left me alone to do what I wanted. At school, however, I had to obey many rules, such as going to bed on time, doing homework, and cleaning up. The older students at our school helped me to see the importance of these rules because that was the tradition at our school: The older students took care of the younger students. The seniors were strict with me when I did something wrong. At first, when they corrected me, I did not obey them. However, I slowly learned that the rules of the school helped me to live easily and well. Going to bed on time meant that I got enough sleep. Doing my homework helped me do well in my studies. Cleaning up made the environment look prettier and also gave me pride in my school. Later, when I had to take care of junior students, I again learned the importance of following rules. I had a difficult time at first because some people didn't want to listen to me and did not follow my orders. As time went on, my juniors learned just as I did, and they became my friends. Even now, we keep in touch and exchange letters.

While staying at school, I learned to be thankful for my parents. The first few years, I got homesick and sometimes cried in bed. I worried that I would

continued

never live with my family again. In addition, many problems of the dorm got me down. At those times, the people who encouraged me to carry on were my parents. Whenever I called them, they gave me confidence because they seemed not to be worried about me. They always said that I should be happy about my situation because only a person who has faced hard times can understand others' feelings. According to my sister, my mother sometimes cried when she was alone because she missed me a lot, but with me, she always tried to be strong. I felt how much they loved and believed in me, so I stopped being unhappy about my situation. Instead, I started thinking about how I could repay their kindness. I decided to try to make their lives happier by doing things they could be proud of.

Slowly, the place I hated became my second home, and it became a memorable stage in my learning about life. I spent the most important period of my life there, growing from a girl to a woman. There, surrounded by other girls, I could build a strong foundation for my life. People who I had a hard time getting along with became my most precious friends. Obeying rules made me a stronger, happier person and a better member of our school community. In addition, I learned how my parents' support contributed to my success and happiness. Whenever I think of these memories, I feel the power and courage to struggle forward through hard times. If we can learn from hard times, they are a rare treasure.

Adapted from an essay by Sayaka Kondo

C Notice the essay structure

EXPLANATORY ESSAYS

An explanatory essay explains or analyzes something that the writer wishes to inform a reader about. The writer has a specific reason for wanting to give the explanation and gives an opinion about the topic. This opinion is supported by examples, details, or other information, so that readers find it convincing.

Practice 1

Answer these questions about "Life Lessons from School." Then discuss your answers with your classmates.

1 What is the topic?
   a high school education in the writer's country
   b how the writer's boarding school experience affected her life
   c the different kinds of friends that the writer made at school

2 What is the writer's opinion about the topic?

3 What sentence in the introduction gives you the topic and the opinion? Underline it twice.

4 What is the writer's reason for explaining this topic?

    a She wants to explain why she was unhappy in school.

    b She wants to convince readers to attend boarding school.

    c She wants to show how attending boarding school changed her.

5 What three things did the writer learn from her experience?

6 Look at the three body paragraphs. Underline the topic sentence in each one.

7 What does the writer do in the conclusion?

    a She discusses some disadvantages of boarding school.

    b She tells about some other things she learned at boarding school.

    c She summarizes the three points she made in the essay.

D Select a topic

TOPICS

When you choose a topic for an explanatory essay, choose one you have a strong opinion about. Good choices are often related to something in your own life, culture, or experience that your classmates don't know about. As you think about your topic, ask yourself these questions.

• What do I want people to understand about me, my country, or my culture?

• What information about me would surprise or interest other people?

After you have chosen your topic, ask these questions to refine and revise your topic.

• Is the topic too broad? (There is too much to write about.)

• Is the topic too narrow? (There is not enough to write about.)

• Is the topic too boring? (It does not seem interesting.)

• Is the topic too factual? (It is mostly facts; there is no strong opinion.)

A good topic is neither too broad nor too narrow.

Practice **2**

Work with a partner. The topics below are for an essay about an important event or person. Describe the problems with each topic and give two revised topics. The first one has been done for you.

Topic	Problem	Revised topics
1 How many cousins I have	*Too narrow – the answer will be very brief.* *Factual – there is no opinion about the cousins*	*What I learned from my cousins* *Why living with an extended family is important to me.*
2 Living abroad		
3 I didn't learn anything from my math teacher.		
4 I felt scared when I missed my plane while on vacation.		
5 Earthquakes		
6 My summer vacation		
7 My soccer coach		

Your turn ✍

Choose a topic from the list below or use one of your own ideas. Refine and revise your topic, asking the questions in the box *Topics* on page 17. Then write your topic on the line.

1 An event that changed my life

2 How I got interested in _____ (hobby or sport)

3 Why people in my country do a certain activity

4 A person who influenced me or whom I admire

5 Why I am studying _____ (your major)

My topic: _____

E Brainstorm

LISTING

Before you can begin to write your essay, you need ideas. One way to get ideas is to brainstorm a list. As you brainstorm your list, don't worry about whether your ideas are good or bad, or whether you will use them in your essay. Just try listing a lot of ideas.

- Write sentences, phrases, or just words.
- Don't worry about spelling or grammar.
- If you don't know a word or phrase in English, try writing it in your native language.
- Write quickly, and write as many ideas as you can.

Later, read the ideas on your list again. Decide which ones you'll probably want to use in your essay. Cross out any ideas that don't seem useful to you, for example, ideas that don't support your thesis statement or examples that aren't interesting enough.

Practice 3

Work with a partner. Look at this brainstormed list of ideas written by the writer of "Life Lessons from School." Compare it to the essay on pages 15–16 and put a check (✓) next to the ideas she used in her essay and an *X* next to the ideas she didn't use. Discuss with your partner why you think she did not use these ideas.

<u>What I learned in boarding school</u>

memories	dormitory
made me a better person	learned to get along with dormitory people
difficult at first — homesick, sad	classes were difficult
expensive for parents	prepared me for college
made good friends	class president
best friend was Sachiko	tennis team
mother was sad, but I didn't know	parents believed in me
parents encouraged me	when I was senior, I took care of juniors
many rules	learned to understand rules

Your turn

Brainstorm a list of ideas related to your topic. See how many ideas you can write down in the box below in five minutes.

F Discuss your ideas with others

With a partner or in a small group, follow these steps to share your ideas and to get new ones.

1 Explain what your topic is and why you chose it.
2 Read from your brainstormed list. Explain how each idea relates to your topic.
3 Answer any questions that your classmates may have about your topic and ideas.
4 Add new ideas to your list.

A Compose the thesis statement

THE THESIS STATEMENT

Just as every paragraph has a topic sentence that tells the main idea of the paragraph, the essay has a *thesis statement* that tells the essay topic and the writer's opinion. The thesis statement is the most important part of the essay and is usually at the end of the introduction.

A strong thesis statement both names the topic and reveals the writer's opinion about that topic. It should be clear and specific. A thesis statement can also list the supporting ideas, but sometimes these are written in a separate sentence.

Look at these examples of a weak and a strong thesis statement.

Weak thesis statement:

India has a lot of interesting festivals.

The statement is too broad – the writer can't discuss all Indian festivals. Even though it does state the writer's opinion, the statement is not clear: It doesn't explain why the festivals are interesting.

Strong thesis statement:

Diwali is an important festival for Indians because they celebrate, remember traditional legends, and enjoy time with their families.

The topic is specific enough, and it clearly gives the writer's opinion. In addition, it lists the supporting ideas.

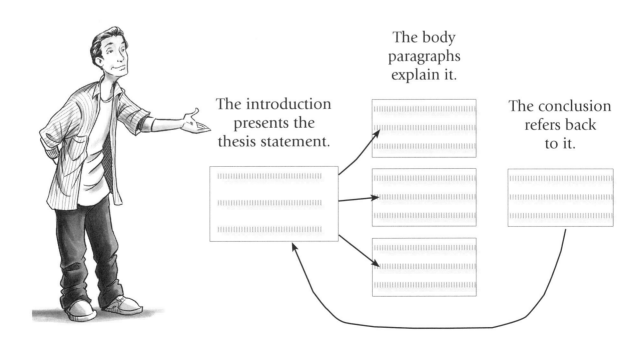

The introduction presents the thesis statement.

The body paragraphs explain it.

The conclusion refers back to it.

Practice 4

Work with a partner. Look at the pairs of thesis statements. Explain why the first thesis statement in each pair is weaker than the second (for example, it doesn't name the topic; it doesn't give the writer's opinion; it isn't clear enough; it is too broad/narrow). See also the box *Topics* on page 17.

1 a I learned a lot from my brother.
  b My brother taught me how to be a better person.

2 a My brother taught me how to be a better person.
  b My brother taught me the value of perseverance, trust, and honesty.

3 a I had a great vacation in Europe!
  b My summer trip to Europe changed me.

4 a My summer trip to Europe changed me.
  b After my summer trip to Europe, I realized the value of a good education.

5 a My family's business failed.
  b My family's business failure was lucky for me.

6 a My family's business failure was lucky for me.
  b Because my family's business failed, I found a wonderful new career.

Practice 5

Look at the following thesis statements. Revise them to make them stronger. Then share your improved thesis statements with a partner.

1 I loved high school.

_____

2 Playing the violin is a good hobby for me.

_____

3 I'll never forget my first boss.

_____

4 New Year's is an important holiday in my country.

_____

5 I had a great part-time job in college.

_____

6 I admire my aunt.

_____

7 My winter vacation was wonderful.

_____

Your turn ↵

Write your thesis statement. Then exchange thesis statements with a partner. Use the questions below to analyze your partner's statement. Then discuss your ideas.

1 Does your partner's thesis statement name the topic?
2 Does it give your partner's opinion?
3 Is it clear and specific?
4 Do you have any comments or suggestions for your partner?

B Edit your brainstorming

Edit your list of brainstormed ideas from *Your turn* on page 20. Follow these steps.

1 Cross out any ideas that you don't like or that do not relate to your thesis statement.
2 Add any new ideas that are related to your thesis statement.
3 Check (✓) the ideas that you like the most.
4 Organize the ideas that you like into related groups of ideas that can be used to support main points in your essay.

C Order ideas

EMPHATIC ORDER

The main points in an essay are often organized according to their importance. Often, less important points are given first. More important points are given later, with the most important point coming last. This is called *emphatic order*. It draws attention to the last, most important point.

First body paragraph	less important point
Second body paragraph	more important point
Final body paragraph	most important point

Practice 6

Read the following points from an explanatory essay about why the writer values his sport, running. Order the points from 1 to 5, with 1 for least important and 5 for most important. Discuss your opinions with a partner. You don't have to agree, but be sure to explain your reasons.

_____ a Competitions encourage me to push myself and do my best.
_____ b Running builds a healthy body.
_____ c Running is a sport that I can do all my life.
_____ d I made my best friends when I joined the track team.
_____ e Running improved my mental concentration.

Your turn ↶

Follow these steps to put your points in order.

1 Choose at least three ideas from part B, *Edit your brainstorming* on page 23.
2 Write each idea – or point – on a separate piece of paper or on index cards.
3 Arrange the slips in order (from least to most important) on your desk.
4 Give the papers to your partner. Have your partner do the same, independently.
5 Compare the order you each chose for the points. Discuss the reason for the order you chose. Do you agree with your partner?
6 Write down your final order for the three most important points. These will be used in your body paragraphs.

D Make an outline

> ### OUTLINING
>
> After you have gathered ideas for your essay, you should write an outline. Writing an outline helps you organize your thoughts and develop a structure for your essay. A well-planned outline ensures that your essay will be well planned and make sense to your audience.
>
> An outline also helps you write your essay because it provides a map of your ideas. You won't forget what you want to say, and you won't accidentally include information that isn't related to your thesis statement and topic sentences.
>
> An outline can be very basic, simply listing the introduction, major points, and conclusion; or it can be more detailed, including specific information for each of the points. In general, an outline that is more detailed offers an easier writing map than a basic outline.

Practice 7

Reread the sample essay "Life Lessons from School" on pages 15–16. Then complete the basic outline of the essay on the next page by writing the sentences below in the correct place.

In boarding school, I learned that I could grow by facing challenges.

I made friends with different kinds of people.

I learned how to make true friends, obey rules, and return my parents' love.

I was thankful for my parents' encouragement and tried to do my best.

I learned why and how to obey rules.

Basic Outline

I. **INTRODUCTION: Thesis statement** _____

_____

II. _____

III. _____

IV. _____

V. **CONCLUSION:** _In boarding school, I learned that I could grow by_ _____

facing challenges.

Practice 8

Read the detailed outline the writer did for the first body paragraph. Complete the missing parts by looking back at the sample essay on pages 15–16.

Detailed Outline

II. **FIRST POINT:** _I learned to make friends with different kinds of people._
    A. Different kinds of people
        1. ages
        2. _____
        3. habits

    B. Getting along
        1. _____
        2. sometimes difficult – had quarrels

    C. Grew to understand each other
        1. shared feelings
            a) _____
            b) _____
            c) rebelliousness
        2. found each other's good points

    D. Became friends
        1. like sisters
        2. still friends now

Your turn ↶

Make an outline for your essay similar to the one on the right. Show your outline to your classmates and discuss the thesis statement. Then discuss the main point of each paragraph. Finally, talk about the order of your paragraphs.

I. INTRODUCTION: Thesis statement
II. FIRST POINT
III. SECOND POINT
IV. THIRD POINT
V. CONCLUSION

E Use transitions

TRANSITIONS

Transitions are words that connect ideas within one sentence or between two sentences.

> Rules were very important at boarding school, <u>so</u> I had to learn how to obey them.
> I didn't like all of the rules. <u>However,</u> I soon learned rules can be helpful.

Coordinating conjunctions are commonly used as transitions to join two independent clauses. An easy way to remember the seven coordinating conjunctions is to think of the word FANBOYS: *<u>F</u>or, <u>A</u>nd, <u>N</u>or, <u>B</u>ut, <u>O</u>r, <u>Y</u>et, <u>S</u>o.*

> I didn't like the rules at first, <u>for</u> I wasn't used to them.
> The rules were sometimes difficult to obey, <u>yet</u> they helped me live a better life.

In academic or formal writing, don't use the coordinating conjunctions *and* or *but* at the beginning of a sentence. Instead, use the transitions *in addition* and *however*.

> **Informal:** I met people of different ages. <u>And</u> I met people from different backgrounds.
> **Formal:** I met people of different ages, <u>and</u> I met people from different backgrounds.
> **Formal:** I met people of different ages. <u>In addition</u>, I met people from different backgrounds.

> **Informal:** Senior students told me the rules. <u>But</u> I didn't obey them.
> **Formal:** Senior students told me the rules, <u>but</u> I didn't obey them.
> **Formal:** Senior students told me the rules. <u>However</u>, I didn't obey them.

Practice 9

Circle the correct transition word.

1 Singing relaxes me, *but* / *so* I sing when I feel troubled or stressed.

2 I don't like cleaning my room, *nor* / *yet* I can do it happily while listening to music.

3 Familiar music is like a message from my family or friends, *so* / *or* it helps stop my loneliness.

4 Karaoke is much cheaper here than back home in my country, *yet* / *so* I go more often here.

5 People all over the world speak different languages, *and* / *but* they all enjoy music.

6 I couldn't live without listening to music, *nor* / *and* could I live without singing.

7 Music blocks out annoying sounds from outside. *And* / *In addition*, it helps me relax, *so* / *but* I always listen to music when I study.

8 I'm sure I will always have music in my life, *for* / *however* I can't imagine living without it.

BECAUSE *AND* THEREFORE

Because and *therefore* are especially useful transitions for explanatory essays. They help the reader understand your explanations by showing causes and results.

<u>Because</u> rules were very important at boarding school, I had to learn how to obey them.
Rules were very important at boarding school. <u>Therefore</u>, I had to learn how to obey them.

Because can come at the beginning or in the middle of a sentence.

<u>Because</u> I was lonely, I sometimes cried at first.
My parents sent me to boarding school <u>because</u> they wanted me to have a good education.

Therefore comes at the beginning of a new sentence.

My parents wanted me to have a good education. <u>Therefore</u>, they sent me to boarding school.

Practice 10

Look at "Life Lessons from School." Circle all of the examples of the FANBOYS conjunctions, *in addition, however, because,* and *therefore*. Where in the sentence do they occur – the beginning? the middle?

Practice 11

Join the two sentences with a transition word. You can write either sentence first. Then share your sentences with a partner or in a small group. Did you ever choose the same transition as your partner or another member of the group?

1 Professor Hayden is a popular instructor. He gives a lot of homework.

_____

2 A part-time job teaches responsibility. It gives you spending money.

_____

3 My parents both worked when I was in school. I had to learn to take care of myself.

_____

4 Playing team sports is supposed to build cooperation and group spirit. I don't like feeling responsible for letting my team down if I make a mistake.

_____

5 In the middle of seventh grade, my family moved to a new city. I was sad to leave my friends behind. I quickly made new friends.

_____

6 On Labor Day, people in the United States honor workers. Workers get a day off to rest on that day.

_____

7 Learning a language is like playing a sport. You have to practice a lot in order to improve.

_____

8 Learning new software applications will help me find a better job. I'm going to take a class at the computer center.

_____

Your turn ✎

Use your outline to write your body paragraphs. In each of your body paragraphs, use at least two transitions. Underline the transitions.

F Write an introduction

THE STRUCTURE OF AN INTRODUCTION

The introduction to an essay begins with the _hook_, a particularly interesting sentence that catches your reader's interest from the beginning.

Follow the hook with some _background_ that explains a little bit about your topic and leads the reader to your thesis statement. The background can give general information or a short history of the topic. Sometimes it is a short personal story that shows why the writer is interested in the topic.

The final part of your introduction will be the _thesis statement_, usually the last sentence in the introduction. See the box _The Thesis Statement_ on page 21.

Practice 12

Look at the introduction on page 29 from "Life Lessons from School." Draw circles around the sentences that form these parts of the introduction and label them: _hook_, _background_, _thesis statement_.

I hated school! Now, however, when I feel discouraged by my problems, I overcome this by trying to remember my years at boarding school. Those years were challenging and full of problems, but still, I gained a lot from them. After I graduated from elementary school, I left my family and went to live at a boarding school because my hometown was very far from my middle school. I stayed there until I graduated from high school. It was very difficult for me at first, but eventually I learned how to make true friends, obey rules, and return my parents' love. Even though these things were not easy to learn, the lessons from my boarding school experience made me an independent woman and a productive member of society.

HOOKS

Hooks can be hard to write. For that reason, some writers don't write the hook until quite late in the writing process. That gives them more time to think of a very strong hook that really grabs their reader's attention. Here are some common hooks.

- A personal experience or idea
  Now, however, when I feel discouraged by my problems, I overcome this by trying to remember my years at boarding school.

- A quotation
  A Czech proverb tells us, "Do not protect yourself by a fence, but rather by your friends."

- A question
  Have you ever wished that you were an only child?

- Surprising information
  Americans make up five percent of the world's population, but use 26 percent of the world's energy.

Practice 13

With a partner or in a small group, read six different hooks for "Life Lessons from School." For each hook, discuss the questions below.

- Which hooks are not effective? Why not?
- Which hooks are effective? What kind of hooks are they (a personal experience, a quotation, a question, surprising information)?
- Which one do you like best?

1 I hated school!

2 Everybody knows about Hogwarts, the famous imaginary boarding school from *Harry Potter*. My boarding school didn't teach us magic, but I still learned many valuable things there.

3 This essay is going to be about what I learned in boarding school.

4 What were the most important things you learned in school? English and math? Science and history? For me, the social education that I received at my boarding school was the most important.

5 Did you go to boarding school? Well, I did.

6 John Adams once said, "There are two types of education. One should teach us how to make a living, and the other how to live." My experience at boarding school taught me both.

Your turn ↶

Write two or three hooks for your introduction. Share them with a partner or in a small group and decide which one you like best. Then write your introductory paragraph with your hook, some background information, and your thesis statement.

G Write a conclusion

THE CONCLUSION

The conclusion ends your essay. You have already made your main points in the body paragraphs, so do not add any new points here. Sometimes in the conclusion you can use the same idea that you used for your introductory hook, but in a different way.

The conclusion summarizes the essay's main points and does one or more of these things:

- makes a prediction
- asks the reader to make some kind of change or take action
- offers a closing thought or comment

Practice 14

Look at the conclusion from the sample essay again. Which of the following does it do? You can check more than one answer.

_____ **a** It reminds the reader of the hook at the beginning of the essay.

_____ **b** It summarizes the essay's main points.

_____ **c** It makes a prediction.

_____ **d** It asks the reader to make some change or take action.

_____ **e** It contains a closing thought or comment.

> Slowly, the place I hated became my second home, and it became a memorable stage in my learning about life. I spent the most important period of my life there, growing from a girl to a woman. There, surrounded by other girls, I could build a strong foundation for my life. People who I had a hard time getting along with became my most precious friends. Obeying rules made me a stronger, happier person and a better member of our school community. In addition, I learned how my parents' support contributed to my success and happiness. Whenever I think of these memories, I feel the power and courage to struggle forward through hard times. If we can learn from hard times, they are a rare treasure.

Practice 15

Work with a partner or in a small group. Reread the original conclusion to "Life Lessons from Boarding School" and three other conclusions. Then discuss the questions below.

- Which conclusion is the weakest? Why is it weak?
- Which one is the strongest? Why? Which introductory hook in *Practice 13* on page 30 does it match?

1   In conclusion, even though boarding school was very difficult for me at first, I learned how to make true friends, obey rules, and return my parents' love.

2   I never used a wand at my boarding school, and I never performed any tricks or spells. However, I did learn magic: I turned strangers into friends, I realized how following strict rules could set me free, and I recognized and understood the love in my family's heart. I will always be grateful that I have these foundations for my life.

3   Another thing I liked about boarding school was the classes. I had very nice teachers, and I learned a lot from them. Therefore, I did well on my college entrance exams. I still send one of my teachers a card at New Year's because I'm so grateful for what I learned. Because of my classes, teachers, friends, and everything else, I'm glad I went to boarding school.

Your turn ↷

Write a conclusion for your essay.

H Write the first draft

As you have worked your way through Section II, you have written all the pieces that you need for an essay: the body paragraphs with transition words, the introduction with a hook and a thesis statement, and the conclusion. Put these pieces together to create the first draft of your essay.

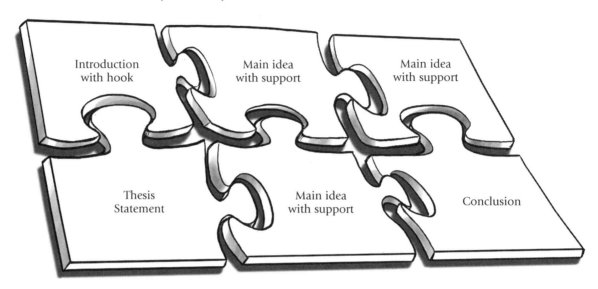

III REVISING YOUR WRITING

A Benefit from peer feedback

USING AND GIVING PEER FEEDBACK

You are writing your essay for a reader. Therefore, it is important to get a reader's reaction before you finish your final draft. A reader can tell you if any parts of your essay are not clear and can let you know which parts were interesting or successful. In addition, you can learn a lot by reading another person's version of a similar assignment. You might notice some different ways of looking at the same assignment.

When you comment on another person's essay, think about how you can be helpful to the writer. Very general comments are not as useful as specific comments that tell the writer what part of the essay was strong or weak and why.

General Comment	**Specific Comment**
This was good – I liked it!	The story about your father's childhood helped me understand his personality.
Your essay wasn't clear, so I couldn't understand it.	I didn't understand what you meant by "the teacher wasn't fair." Can you explain how he wasn't fair, or give an example?

Exchange essays and books with a partner. Fill out the form below about your partner's essay. Then return the book and discuss your answers.

PEER FEEDBACK FORM

Writer's name: _____   Date: _____

Reviewer's name: _____

1 Answer these questions about the introduction. Mark each box ✓ or X .
   ☐ Does the introduction have an interesting hook?
   ☐ Does the introduction include background information?
   ☐ Is the thesis statement in the introduction?

2 On your partner's essay, underline the thesis statement <u>twice</u>.

3 Answer these questions about the thesis statement. Mark each box ✓ or X .
   ☐ Does the thesis statement tell you the topic?
   ☐ Does the thesis statement tell you the writer's opinion?

4 Underline the topic sentence of each body paragraph.

5 Did you understand the explanation in each body paragraph? If not, write the number of the paragraph(s) you didn't understand here: _____

6 Answer these questions about the conclusion. Mark each box ✓ or X .
   ☐ Does the conclusion summarize the writer's main points?
   ☐ Does the conclusion make any new main points?
   ☐ Does the conclusion refer back to the hook or introduction?

7 On the essay, draw a star (★) in the margin by your favorite sentences. Choose two or three.

8 Were there any sentences you didn't understand? If so, write a question mark (?) in the margin next to the sentence.

9 Look for transitions such as FANBOYS, *in addition, however, because,* and *therefore.* Circle them. How many of these transitions did the writer use? _____

10 Any other comments: _____

_____

_____

B Title your essay

TITLES

Just as every book has a title, every essay should have a title. A title does not need to be long; however, it should catch the reader's interest. Remember, a title is the first thing that the reader reads.

Writing a title is a bit of an art. Don't be discouraged if it takes several tries to write a title that pleases you. When you write your essay title, keep these points in mind.

- It may be just a few words (but it could be longer).
- It should summarize the subject, or focus, of your essay.
- A title may hint at the essay's purpose.
- Titles should be catchy – that is they should catch the reader's attention.
- Titles are usually not a complete sentence.
- Capitalize only the main words of the title, not the articles and prepositions. Always capitalize the first word of a title.

Practice 16

Look at these different possible titles for the sample essay on pages 15–16. Which titles do you like? Which is your favorite? Share your opinions about each title with a partner.

1 Boarding School
2 Life Lessons from School
3 When I Have Children, I'm Going to Send Them to Boarding School Because I Learned So Much There When I Was in School
4 Life: The Most Important Subject
5 A Modern Hogwarts: My Path to Maturity
6 Things I Learned in School
7 The Advantages of Boarding School

Your turn ↶

Look at your essay. Does it have a title? Are you satisfied with it? If not, write two or three more possible titles here. Then talk with your peer feedback partner about which one you like best.

C Critical thinking

> ## *REVISING*
>
> Revising includes rereading and checking your essay and making any necessary changes. You might add more information to make a point clearer. Or you might delete details that are not relevant. You might even rewrite an explanation to make it easier to understand.
>
> Of course, the information about your topic is clear in your mind. But is it also clear in your essay? Your audience may not be familiar with the topic you have chosen. So, when you reread your draft before revising, think critically about everything that you have written. Make sure that all your explanations are logical and complete. Following your topic sentences, your body paragraphs should answer any questions that might arise in the reader's mind, such as *how?* and *why?*

Practice 17

Work with a partner and read the three paragraphs. For each paragraph, discuss the questions below.

- What point is the paragraph trying to explain?
- How well does the paragraph explain that point?
- What (if anything) needs to be added, deleted, or rewritten to explain the point more effectively?

1   My brother is a very hard worker. He always works hard. In addition, he is successful at his work. I really admire that. I hope when I grow up that I can be a good worker like my brother. If I want to do that, I will have to work very hard.

2   My brother gave me a good example of how a son should behave. He was always kind to my parents, and he helped them with housework and yard work. He never disobeyed them, but instead he always carried out their orders cheerfully. My father traveled frequently, and he depended on my brother to take care of us. My brother always did a good job, so my father didn't worry when he traveled. Because he always behaved well, my brother honored my parents and our family name.

3   My brother is more than just a relative to me. He is my friend. Our friendship is very important to me. I know some people who do not even like their brothers! I can't believe that. My brother is one of my best friends, even though he is my brother. When I was a child, I always had a friend near me because I lived with my brother.

Your turn ↶

Think critically about your body paragraphs. What questions does your reader need answered? Do you answer those questions with complete explanations? If you need to make any changes, write notes on your essay.

D Make revision decisions

Reread your essay and think about your partner's peer feedback. Mark any changes that you want to make on your paper.

E Write the second draft

Use the notes you wrote on your first draft to make revisions. Write the second draft of your essay.

IV EDITING YOUR WRITING

A Punctuate transitions

PUNCTUATION WITH FANBOYS

All of the FANBOYS transitions – *for, and, not, but, or, yet, so* – follow the same rules for punctuation:

If they connect two complete sentences (each one has a subject and a verb), a comma is used before the transition:

S V   S   V
I made good friends in boarding school. I still keep in touch with them.

S V   S   V
I made good friends in boarding school, and I still keep in touch with them.

Don't use a comma if the second clause uses the same subject as the first, and it doesn't repeat that subject:

S V   V
I made good friends in boarding school and still keep in touch with them.

Practice 18

Connect each pair of sentences to make one sentence using the transition in parentheses. Use correct punctuation.

1 My family hosted a foreign exchange student. I wanted to study abroad too. (*so*)

_____

2 I had to quit the team. I had to improve my grades. (*or*) (Note: Remove the subject in the second clause.)

_____

3 I couldn't follow what he was saying. He was talking too quickly. (*for*)

_____

4 My father lost his job. He didn't become discouraged. (*yet*)

_____

5 My parents told me I looked fine. I had no confidence in my appearance. (*but*)

_____

6 My father found out I had told a lie. He punished me for it. (*and*) (Note: Remove the subject in the second clause.)

_____

PUNCTUATION WITH OTHER TRANSITIONS

When you use the transitions *in addition*, *however*, and *therefore* at the beginning of a sentence, use a comma after them:

> In addition, I sometimes visit my old school.

When you use *because* in the middle of a sentence, you usually don't need a comma:

> I respect my brother because he is such a hard worker.

When you use *because* at the beginning of a sentence, use a comma after the first part of the sentence:

> Because my brother is such a hard worker, I respect him.

Practice 19

Connect each pair of sentences below with the transition in parentheses. Use correct punctuation. Some sentences can be connected in more than one way. Then compare your sentences with a partner.

1 Everybody liked my uncle. He was funny and kind. (*because*)

_____

2 Movies taught me a lot about far-off places. They taught me about different kinds of people. (*in addition*)

_____

3 I wanted to find a job in sales. I didn't have any experience. (*yet*)

_____

4 Some computer games teach children how to think. These games should be considered educational. (*therefore*)

_____

5 There have been many accidents at that intersection. The city should install a traffic light. (*because*)

---

6 Many students study computer programming in college. There are not enough jobs for all of them. (*however*)

---

7 I want to study French or German. I can travel easily in Europe. (*so*)

Practice 20

Read the following paragraph from a student's essay on the advantages of attending public schools. Edit for correct comma usage with transitions. There are nine errors. The first one is marked for you.

A second advantage of attending a public school was meeting many different kinds of people. The children in my neighborhood were similar to me. Our parents had similar types of jobs, and we lived in similar houses. However at my school, I met children from richer, and poorer families. Some children lived in apartments, or on farms. I learned to get along with many different kinds of children so I can get along with many kinds of people today. Because, private schools in my country cost a lot of money, only rich children can go there. Therefore children at private schools don't interact with poorer children. However it is important to learn to interact with all kinds of people for you will meet them at some point in your life.

Your turn

Check the transitions in your essay. Did you punctuate them correctly?

B Write the final draft

Write the final draft. As you write, make sure that your spelling, punctuation, and formatting are correct; and check for any grammar errors.

A Share your writing

Work in a small group (3–5 students). Share your essay by following these steps.

1 Read aloud just the introduction of your essay. See if the other students can predict the topics of your body paragraphs. Read your introduction a second time if necessary.

2 When you have finished sharing your introductions, turn to the person on your left and give him or her one compliment on the introduction (for example, "Your hook was interesting" or "Your thesis statement was very clear").

B Check your progress

After you get your essay back from your instructor, complete the *Progress Check* below.

PROGRESS CHECK
Date: _____
Essay title: _____
Things I did well in this essay:
_____
_____
_____
Things I need to work on in my next essay:
_____
_____
_____

Problem-Solution Essays

Everyone faces problems. Some problems are small, such as having to find the best way to get from one place to another and avoid heavy traffic. Others may be much larger, such as a financial or a relationship problem.

In this chapter, you will write an essay in which you identify a problem and then propose a possible solution. You will practice the critical thinking that is necessary to solve a problem effectively.

A Think about the sample essay topic

You are going to read an essay by a writer who feels that sleep-deprived students in her school cause a problem. The writer then proposes a solution to this problem. Before you read the essay, look at the information below and answer the questions that follow.

Figure 2.1 Behavior of students depending on amount of sleep

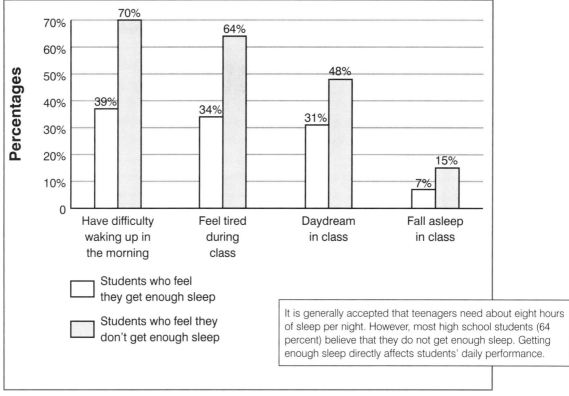

Source: The Harris Poll® 2003

1 According to Figure 2.1, if a student feels that she doesn't get enough sleep, how is this likely to affect her performance in school?

2 How much sleep do you get each night? Do you feel you get enough sleep?

3 How do you feel when you don't get enough sleep? How does it affect your work or schoolwork?

4 Have you ever been distracted by a sleepy classmate?

5 Is lack of sleep a problem for students in your school? Why or why not? Can you think of any way that a school could help solve the problem?

B Read the sample essay

As you read the sample essay, ask yourself if the writer has convinced you that there is a serious problem and if the solution she offers is reasonable. Then share your ideas with a partner.

Eight Hours a Night

In my classes, sleep-deprived students tend to disturb other students, and this can make it hard to learn. No matter what class they are in, sleep-deprived students are likely to cause problems. For example, they rarely contribute to the classroom topic. If they do say anything in class, it's usually just to answer a question that was already answered. Such sleepy students can even kill motivation for students who are awake. When I see five people sleeping with their heads on top of their desks, it is possible that I will feel sleepy too, especially if it is a boring or an early morning class. Another problem with many students who don't get enough sleep is that it is not unusual for them to arrive late to class, interrupting whatever is happening. To solve these problems, I think that teachers should make sleep a part of the class requirement.

The sleep requirement should be like any other activity that students are graded on, such as homework, attendance, tests, or participation. In my opinion, the sleep requirement should be eight hours a night, since this is how much sleep an average person tends to need. In order to achieve this number, students will keep a record of their sleep every night. Then every week students will give their records to their teacher and receive a grade for them. Teachers can also use other grading policies to strengthen the sleep requirement. For instance, any student who sleeps in class will lose ten points from their participation grade. Students who are late will not be allowed in the classroom, and again, they will lose points. At the end of the semester, the teacher will count those weekly "sleep" grades as part of the final course grade. If students know that sleeping will have an effect on their final grade, they will surely take sleep more seriously.

A sleep requirement might be seen by many people, especially students, as a student's personal responsibility. But what about dress codes and language? Even though these elements are very personal, many schools have rules about acceptable dress and language. Schools set expectations for students in many ways, from homework requirements to dress and language codes, to rules about bad behavior in class. These expectations and rules relate to a variety of elements that support the learning environment. Clearly, this includes rules about coming to class rested. If a school sets high expectations about behavior, students will be more likely to work to reach those expectations.

Students who do not get enough sleep can cause many problems in school. Not only is their own learning limited, but also their behavior affects the entire classroom negatively. All educational systems should consider the fact that sleep-deprived students can affect both their own and their peers' level of academic achievement. Teachers should motivate students

continued

to get enough sleep by making a sleep requirement and by making sure that students obey it. This is no different from many other types of rules that students routinely follow in order to get a high level of academic performance. If teachers show that they value rested students, it is probable that students will value their rest more too. This will also improve the school experience of all students.

Adapted from a composition by Melissa Carrasco

C Notice the essay structure

PROBLEM-SOLUTION ESSAYS

In a problem-solution essay, the writer first explains a problem (the topic) and then proposes a solution or solutions. The writer needs to persuade the reader that the problem is important, and that the solution is reasonable. The solution should be practical and achievable.

Practice 1

Answer these questions about "Eight Hours a Night." Then discuss your answers with your classmates.

1 In the essay, where is the problem described?
   a in the first paragraph
   b in the second paragraph
   c near the end of the essay

2 What is the problem? Is the problem relevant or interesting to you as the reader?

3 Find the thesis statement, and underline it twice. What solution does it propose?

4 In the first body paragraph, the writer explains how a teacher would put this solution into action. Is the explanation effective? Why or why not?

5 In the second body paragraph, the writer describes why setting a sleep requirement is reasonable. What is the writer's argument?
   a Students are more responsible when they are given instructions.
   b By setting standards, schools can influence students' behavior in positive ways.
   c A school should not set standards about students' personal lives.

6 Does the writer's argument convince you? Why or why not?

7 The conclusion restates main ideas that have been discussed in the essay. Find two ideas in the essay body that are restated in the conclusion. Compare the wording of the ideas in the essay with the wording in the conclusion.

8 Do you think the solution suggested in the essay will help to solve the problem of students not getting enough sleep? Why or why not? What other solutions can you think of that might be effective?

D Select a topic

CHOOSING A TOPIC

When you choose a topic for a problem-solution essay, think of a problem that you or somebody you know has had. If you have had this problem, it is likely that others have had it too.

- Choose a problem that affects you, and be sure that you have a strong opinion about it.
- Choose a problem that is relevant or interesting to your readers.
- Make sure that you have a reasonable solution for the problem.

Practice 2

Read the following topics. Evaluate each topic according to the listed criteria. Check (✓) the criteria that you think each topic meets.

Possible essay topic	Is the problem relevant to you?	Do you have a strong opinion about it?	Is the problem relevant or interesting to your readers?	Can you propose a reasonable solution?
1 Some students bully other students at school.				
2 Writing essays in English is really hard.				
3 Most parents prefer to hire a female babysitter.				
4 When students or workers do a group project, they are evaluated according to others' work.				
5 Students watch TV and use the Internet while they are doing their homework.				
6 Finding a good job is difficult to do.				

Your turn ↵

Choose a topic from the list below.

1 Sixteen-year-old drivers cause a lot of car accidents.

2 Sticking to a diet or exercise routine seems impossible to do.

3 Shy people can find it difficult to meet or socialize with others.

4 Many schools don't have any club or organization for their international students.

5 So many people put off till tomorrow what they should do today.

6 Other topic: _____

E Brainstorm

FREEWRITING

Freewriting means writing anything that comes into your mind about your topic. Good freewriting is truly free, so do not worry about grammar or spelling. The purpose of freewriting is to brainstorm as many ideas as you can. If you get stuck, force yourself to write something – anything. You can even write the same word or phrase over and over until a new idea comes to you. Set a time limit, such as five or ten minutes, and just keep writing until the time is up.

Practice 3

Read a student's freewriting about the problem of overweight children in the United States. Underline any solutions.

> Children in America are getting really fat. It's a shameful problem. Some people in the world are starving, and Americans are eating too much. Many reasons for their weight problems. First, they eat too much. They should eat less. At restaurants in America, they serve huge portions. Nobody can finish it. Need smaller portions, eat until full. What is the prize for eating a big meal? Dessert. Dessert, sweets, candy, cookies. Should eat less sugar!

Candy is a prize in a lot of situations. Ex: Some schools give candy as a prize for doing homework or winning a competition. Food shouldn't be a prize. Another big problem is snacking. Kids always snack . . . home, school, camp. Too many snacks! American kids snack all of the time — libraries, bus stops, parking lots, cars, movies, watching TV. Bad eating habits. Need meals, not snacks. When they get older, they will continue with these bad habits. Start good eating habits young. Should sit down and eat healthy meals. Americans eat while they walk down the street. In my country, this is socially unacceptable. Eating is one problem, but no exercise is the next reason. Kids sit around too much. Watch TV. Drive everywhere. No walking or biking. When we visit my parents' country, everybody is walking or biking. In America, most of my friends have video game systems, computers, and TVs in their bedroom. Even keep snacks in their bedroom! Schools don't help. Gym class is only once or twice a week. Need more sports!

Your turn ↷

Follow these steps to brainstorm about your topic.

1 Freewrite about your topic. Write for five minutes. Write everything that comes to mind and don't worry about grammar or spelling.
2 When you finish, reread your freewriting. Underline words and phrases that could be part of the solution.

F Discuss your ideas with others

With a partner or in a small group, follow these steps to share your ideas and get new ones.

1 Explain what your topic is (the problem) and why you chose it.
2 Read your freewriting aloud. Encourage your classmates to ask questions or add thoughts.
3 Explain your solution(s) to the problem. Explain how the solution(s) would work.
4 Ask your classmates if they have any other possible solutions to your problem.
5 Listen to your classmates share their experiences or information about your topic. Consider their points of view.
6 Write down any new ideas from your discussion.

A Organize the essay

THE STRUCTURE OF A PROBLEM-SOLUTION ESSAY

Problem-solution essays typically follow one of two patterns depending on whether the writer offers several ways or one way to solve the problem. In each case, the introduction describes the problem. However, the organization of the body in each type is different.

In Type 1, each body paragraph describes a different way to solve the problem. In Type 2, usually the first body paragraph gives a detailed description of the solution and how it will work. The other body paragraphs may vary. One may give reasons why the solution will work; another may describe the benefits of the solution; a third may compare the solution to a more common solution; and so on.

- **Type 1: Several solutions**
Introduction	Problem
Paragraph	One way to solve the problem
Paragraph	A second way to solve the problem
Paragraph	Another way to solve the problem
Conclusion	

- **Type 2: One solution**
Introduction	Problem
Paragraph	Description of the solution
Paragraph	More information about the solution
Paragraph	More information about the solution
Conclusion	

Practice 4

Work with a partner. Read the outlines for two problem-solution essays on the next page and answer the following questions.

1 Which outline is for a Type 1 essay?
   a "Keeping the 'Little' in 'Little People'"
   b "Malls and Teens Meet in the Middle"

2 For the Type 2 essay, match each of the body paragraphs (II, III, and IV) with one of the following:
   a It compares the solution to another solution.
   b It explains the benefits of the solution.
   c It gives a detailed description of the solution.

Outline for "Keeping the 'Little' in 'Little People'"

I. American children are often overweight. In order to stay healthy, they need to change several common lifestyle habits.

II. Children should eat three or four times a day, instead of snacking constantly, eating on the run, and having candy as a treat or a prize.

III. Children should eat smaller portions at their main meals.

IV. Children should do fewer seated activities such as watching TV and do more physical activities.

V. Conclusion

Outline for "Malls and Teens Meet in the Middle"

I. Problem: On Friday and Saturday nights, a lot of teenagers gather at the local shopping mall to socialize. They make noise, hang out in front of specific stores, and create garbage, but they don't usually shop much. The mall wants to prohibit teens from coming to the mall without their parents after 7 p.m.

Solution: The mall should hire "teen guards" to patrol the malls and inspire better behavior from teens.

II. Teen guards know how to communicate with other teens and could help improve communication among teens, merchants, and mall staff.

III. Teen mall guards would work like hall guards at school, mostly to inspire good behavior, but also with some authority. Also, they would be paid.

IV. Hiring teen guards is friendlier than prohibiting teens in malls, and it's cheaper than hiring armed adult guards.

V. Conclusion

Your turn

Think about your solution(s). Are you proposing several solutions to your problem, or just one? Decide which organization your essay will follow: Type 1 (several solutions) or Type 2 (one solution).

B Plan the introduction

> ### INTRODUCTION TO A PROBLEM-SOLUTION ESSAY
>
> The introductory paragraph to a problem-solution essay usually describes a problem. It begins with a hook, tells what the problem is, when it's a problem, who or what causes the problem, who is affected by the problem and how. These details give the reader the background information that is needed to understand the problem. The final part of the introduction is often the thesis statement, and it introduces the solution(s) that are presented in the body paragraphs.

Practice 5

Work with a partner or in a small group. Read the following introduction to "Malls and Teens Meet in the Middle." Then answer the questions.

> Malls want shoppers, but they may not want you. The local shopping mall is considering kicking out its teenage shoppers. Store owners in the mall argue that teenagers create a lot of disturbances, and the result is a bad shopping environment for other mall-goers. According to some store managers, teenagers make a lot of noise, they leave garbage around, and their behavior is unruly, especially on weekend evenings. To solve this problem, the mall owners are considering excluding teenage shoppers unless they come with their parents. However, a much friendlier solution is to bring teen patrols into the malls on weekend evenings.

1 Is there a hook?
2 What is the problem?
3 When and where is it a problem?
4 Who or what causes the problem?
5 Who is affected by the problem?
6 What is the solution?

Your turn

Plan your introduction. Think about some possible hooks. Consider what information you need in order to describe your problem. Share your ideas with a partner and think of ways to develop them.

C Compose the thesis statement

Practice 6

Work with a partner. Decide which of the following would make a good thesis statement for an essay based on the outline "Keeping the 'Little' in 'Little People'" on page 49.

1 American children are overweight because of lifestyle habits that they need to change.
2 Since American children are overweight, they should eat regular meals instead of snacking constantly, eating on the go, and seeing candy as a reward.
3 In order to maintain a healthy weight, American children need to change many lifestyle habits related to when they eat, how much they eat, and how much physical activity they get.
4 Three unhealthy habits are making American children overweight: eating snacks between meals, eating huge portions, and doing too many seated activities.

Your turn ↶

Write your introductory paragraph with your hook, a description of the problem, and your thesis statement.

D Make an outline

Practice **7**

Before the writer of "Eight Hours a Night" wrote her essay, she wrote the outline below. However, while she was writing, she changed some of her ideas. Compare the original outline below to the final essay on pages 43–44 and answer the questions that follow. Discuss your ideas with a partner.

Outline for "Eight Hours a Night"

I. **Introduction with Thesis Statement:** Sleepy students hurt learning in class, so teachers should require sleep.

II. **First main idea:** A sleep requirement should be assigned and graded like any other coursework.
   A. Like homework, attendance
   B. 8 hours
   C. Daily sleep record is recorded

III. **Second main idea:** "Class participation" isn't enough.
   A. Teachers grade class participation, should include sleep
   B. Lose points for late arrival or sleeping in class

IV. **Third main idea:** Teachers should set high expectations.
   A. Dress codes, language
   B. Students follow rules
   C. Grades show what is valued and expected
   D. Sleep is not just personal

V. **Conclusion**

---

1 The writer decided that one of the paragraphs in her outline was weak and that she didn't want to keep it. Which paragraph was it?

_____

2 The writer decided, however, to keep one idea from the weak paragraph and put it in a different paragraph. What idea was it? Where did she put it?

_____

3 The writer also softened one of her ideas in section IV of her outline to reflect how students really behave. Which idea was it?

_____

Your turn ✍

Make an outline for your essay similar to the one on the right. Include your thesis statement and the main idea for each of the body paragraphs. Add details and examples that support the main idea in each paragraph. Reread your freewriting to help prompt your thinking.

I. INTRODUCTION: Thesis statement
II. FIRST MAIN IDEA
III. SECOND MAIN IDEA
IV. THIRD MAIN IDEA
V. CONCLUSION

E Plan the conclusion

THE CONCLUSION

In a problem-solution essay, the conclusion often mentions the problem again. Then it summarizes the solution(s) that were discussed in the essay. In a problem-solution essay, the final closing sentence in the conclusion often comments optimistically about the success of the solution.

Practice 8

Reread the concluding paragraph in "Eight Hours a Night." Notice the last sentence, which is the closing sentence. Read some other possible closing sentences on page 54. Which could complete this essay nicely? Discuss your answers with a partner.

> Students who do not get enough sleep can cause many problems in school. Not only is their own learning limited, but also their behavior affects the entire classroom negatively. All educational systems should consider the fact that sleep-deprived students can affect both their own and their peers' level of academic achievement. Teachers should motivate students to get enough sleep by making a sleep requirement and by making sure that students obey it. This is no different from many other types of rules that schools routinely follow in order to get a high level of academic performance. If teachers show that they value rested students, it is probable that students will value their rest more too. This will improve the school experience of all students.

_____ **1** Everybody should know it.

_____ **2** If students aren't sleepy in class, I won't be so distracted by them.

_____ **3** I will be lucky if I can get enough sleep every night.

_____ **4** When students are rested and teachers are happy, the whole school will benefit.

Your turn

Plan your conclusion. Reread your introduction, outline, and thesis statement to make sure that the conclusion ties directly to the problem and solution(s) that you've written about.

F Discuss your ideas with others

Get together in a small group with students who wrote about the same problem you did. Share your introductions and outlines. Follow these steps.

1 Discuss the introductory paragraph. Does it state the problem? Does it propose a solution?

2 Discuss the details and support for each main idea. Is the support appropriate and relevant? Can you think of other information that would support the writer's main ideas?

3 Do you think the solution (or solutions) will work? Why or why not?

G Write the first draft

As you have worked your way through Section II, you have written most elements that you need for a problem-solution essay: an introduction and thesis, main ideas about the solution, and support for those ideas. Put these pieces together to create the first draft of your essay. As you write, be open to new ways of thinking about the problem and solution. Add a conclusion that summarizes your main points.

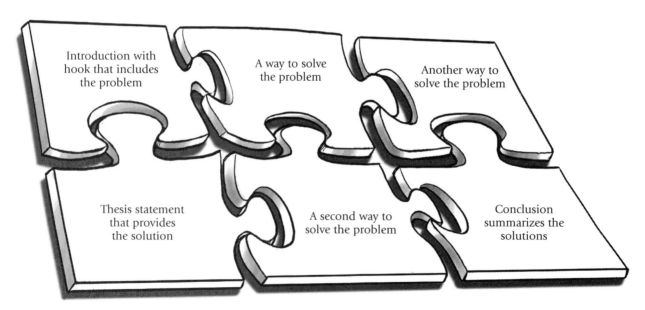

A Benefit from peer feedback

Exchange essays and books with a partner. Fill out the form below about your partner's essay. Then return the book and discuss your answers.

PEER FEEDBACK FORM

Writer's name: _____   Date: _____

Reviewer's name: _____

1 What is the problem that is discussed in the essay?
   _____

2 On your partner's paper, underline the thesis statement twice.

3 Answer these questions about the introduction. Mark each box ✓ or X.
   ☐ Is there an interesting hook?
   ☐ Is there a description of the problem?
   ☐ Does the thesis statement mention the solution(s)?

4 Underline the topic sentence of each body paragraph.

5 Is this a Type 1 (several solutions) or a Type 2 (one solution) problem-solution essay? _____

6 Look at the writer's original outline for this essay. Compare the outline to the essay. Do you see any differences between the two? Can you see any areas where the writer's ideas may have changed during writing?
   _____

7 Answer these questions about the conclusion. Mark each box ✓ or X.
   ☐ Does the conclusion summarize the main points of the essay?
   ☐ Are any new points added?
   ☐ Does the conclusion contain a recommendation, a prediction, or a closing thought?
   ☐ Does the conclusion tie back to the introduction?

8 Draw a star (★) in the margin next to your favorite sentences. Choose two or three.

9 Any other comments: _____
   _____
   _____

B Include your reader

An essay can use techniques that appeal to the reader, just like an ad on T. V.

Practice 9

Read the two introductory paragraphs. Then discuss the questions that follow with a partner.

Introduction A

My job last year wore me out. The only thing that kept me going was the thought of my summer vacation. However, my vacation was even more hectic than my job. I tried to go swimming, sailing, fishing, and hiking in the same day. I got so tired! Then I spent some time with my relatives, but it wasn't relaxing at all. I have a lot of young cousins, nephews, and nieces, and they just wore me out. I should have stayed at a hotel. Furthermore, I tried to see three museums in one day and then went out dancing at night. I was exhausted the next day! Next time, I think I'll just go swimming and sailing on one day and go fishing or hiking the next day. I am now convinced that people on vacation should limit their scheduled activities.

Introduction B

Is relaxation an important part of your vacation? It is for most people – they just want to relax. After all, many people take trips to get away from the hustle and stress of everyday life. However, if you talk to them after they return, you may often learn that their vacation gave them little chance to relax. Indeed, many people plan action-packed getaways that create more stress and fatigue than relaxation. To achieve their purpose of relaxing during their vacation, travelers should consider limiting their scheduled activities in order to allow themselves truly free time.

1 Which introduction does a better job of including you, the reader?
2 In the better paragraph, what language and techniques does the writer use to include the reader?
3 In the weaker paragraph, how could the writer revise it to better include the reader?

Your turn ↜

Look at your essay and ask yourself these questions. Then make notes about revising your essay as needed.

- Does your essay relate to your readers?
- Do you directly show readers how the problem is relevant to them?
- Do you directly tie readers' interest to your solution?

C Think critically

EVALUATING SOLUTIONS

When you write about solutions to a problem, it is important to think critically about the solution you are proposing. Will it really solve the problem? Will it solve the problem completely? Will it always, or just sometimes, fix the problem?

For example, research shows that smoking tobacco can cause some types of cancer. A student wishing to address the problem of cancer may, therefore, suggest solving the problem of cancer by making tobacco illegal. But is this sentence true?

If people don't smoke, they won't get cancer.

This is inaccurate. People can still get cancer from other sources, and of course sometimes the source of cancer cannot be determined at all. It would be more accurate for the student to write:

If people don't smoke, their risk of cancer is smaller.

Practice 10

Work with a partner. Discuss the sentences below. Check (✓) if they are OK or inaccurate. Rewrite any inaccurate sentences. Then share your rewritten sentences with another pair or the class.

1 If you get good grades in school, you will get a good job.

_____ OK

___✓___ inaccurate

If you get good grades in school, you are more likely to get a good job.

2 Exercising may keep children from gaining too much weight.

_____ OK

_____ inaccurate

_____

3 Driving more slowly leads to fewer road accidents.

_____ OK

_____ inaccurate

_____

4 If students don't play video games, they'll make more friends.

_____ OK

_____ inaccurate

_____

5 Cutting up all your credit cards will keep you out of debt.

_____ OK

_____ inaccurate

_____

6 Rested students get higher grades.

_____ OK

_____ inaccurate

_____

7 If a boy is on a sports team, he will be popular.

_____ OK

_____ inaccurate

_____

8 Smoking causes cancer.

_____ OK

_____ inaccurate

_____

9 Writing a few drafts of an essay may improve its organization.

_____ OK

_____ inaccurate

_____

Your turn ↶

Check your essay. Think critically about the solution or solutions in your essay. Are they accurate? Mark any changes that you would like to make on your paper.

D Make revision decisions

Reread your essay and think about your partner's peer feedback. Also consider how well you included your reader in your essay and how accurate your solutions are. Mark any changes that you want to make on your paper.

E Write the second draft

Use the notes you wrote on your first draft to make revisions. Write the second draft of your essay.

A Use hedging to avoid overgeneralization

HEDGING

Rarely in life do we know something or can state something with one hundred percent certainty, especially when we are proposing a solution to a difficult problem. Still, when we are speaking, we are often careless and say things like:

"This will/won't happen."
"This always/never happens."
"Everyone/no one does this."

In writing, however, it is important to make claims that you can defend as true. To do this, you often need to use hedging language. When you hedge, you avoid overgeneralizing. You limit how certain you are about something, and this tells the reader that you are a reasonable writer whose statements can be trusted.

There are many ways to hedge. A few are listed here.

Use qualifying phrases such as:
It is likely that . . . ; it is unlikely that . . . ; it is possible that . . . ;
it would seem that . . . ; . . . tend to . . .

Use the following modals, but avoid *will* and *won't*:
can, could, may, might, should

Use the following modifiers, but avoid *all, every, no*:
a few, a great deal, a large number, many, most, some

Use the following adverbs, but avoid *always* and *never*:
approximately, sometimes, usually, generally, often, possibly, probably, perhaps, in many cases, frequently, rarely

It is quite likely that academic writers may have a tendency to state their ideas in a way that occasionally might make it appear as though they may not be quite sure that what they seem to be saying may or may not be true.

Practice 11

Reread the first paragraph of the essay "Eight Hours a Night." Find ten examples of hedging language and circle them. Compare your answers with a partner. The first one is done for you as an example.

In my classes, sleep-deprived students (tend to) disturb other students, and this can make it hard to learn. No matter what class they are in, sleep-deprived students are likely to cause problems. For example, they rarely contribute to the classroom topic. If they do say anything in the class, it's usually just to answer a question that was already answered. Such sleepy students can even kill motivation for students who are awake. When I see five people sleeping with their heads on top of their desks, it is possible that I will feel sleepy too, especially if it is a boring or an early morning class. Another problem with many students who don't get enough sleep is that it is not unusual for them to arrive late to class, interrupting whatever is happening. To solve these problems, I think that teachers should make sleep a part of the class requirement.

Practice 12

Add the hedging word or words in parentheses to the sentence to avoid making a generalization that may not be true. If necessary, make other changes to the sentences to make them grammatically correct.

1 Putting a television in a child's bedroom is $\overset{somewhat}{\wedge}$ dangerous; $\overset{most}{\wedge}$ children are unable to control how much TV they watch. (*somewhat; most*)

2 After giving birth, women face challenges in controlling their weight. (*a large number of; may*)

3 Students who carry heavy backpacks will experience back troubles. (*many; are likely to*)

4 People in my company work overtime. (*quite a few; frequently*)

5 My classmates say that they listen to music while doing their homework. (*most of; tend to*)

6 Climbers at those altitudes will run out of breath and need to breathe from an oxygen tank. (*it is possible that; some*)

7 Experts believe that diet soda is just as bad for your health as regular soda. (*many; probably*)

8 Shy students never contribute to class discussions. (*it seems that; rarely*)

Practice 13

Rewrite the following sentences to show hedging.

1 Eating a large breakfast will improve students' performance during the day.

_____

2 Drinking more than three cups of coffee a day is bad for your health.

_____

3 Students who can't get parking permits on campus will take the bus.

_____

4 Putting five copies of each course book on reserve in the library will help students save money on textbooks.

_____

5 Every student complains about the complicated course registration process.

_____

Your turn ↶

Check your second draft. Are there any generalizations? If they seem too broad, add language to soften them. Examine any statements that may sound stronger than is justified. Hedge where appropriate. Mark changes on your paper.

B Use conditionals to hedge

USING CONDITIONALS TO HEDGE

Conditional sentences are useful when writing about solutions because they express predictions. They say what _may, might, could,_ or _will_ happen if you take a certain course of action. In one common conditional sentence, the _if_-clause often uses the simple present, even though the time is really future, and the main clause uses future time (_will, be going to_):

       if-clause   main clause
If you don't study for the test, you will surely fail.

This sentence states its prediction with a fair degree of certainty. However, in many cases, the writer may not want to express so much certainty. Where the predictability of the result is less certain, you can use modals to _hedge_ in the main clause.

  If the teacher gives a 15-minute break, students <u>might take</u> 20 minutes.
  If you sit near the front of the class, you <u>may be</u> less likely to fall asleep.

Practice 14

Circle the expression that shows less certainty about the prediction. Discuss your answers with your classmates.

1 If those students turn in identical essays, the teacher *will want / may want* to talk to them after class.

2 Students *might be / will be* late to the assembly if the bus arrives late to school.

3 If you can't commit to team practice on Thursdays, you *won't be /* you *may not be* able to compete in all of the games.

4 If Anna forgets her password again, the bank *will / could* simply refuse to give her another ATM card.

5 You *will get /* You *may get* a better grade if you do the extra credit assignments.

6 If you don't eat breakfast, you *will / may feel* tired in the afternoon.

Practice 15

Complete the sentences with *will, may, might,* or *could.* Pay attention to your verb tenses and your degree of certainty.

1 If you drive steadily at just below the speed limit all the time, <u>you will avoid getting a speeding ticket.</u>

2 If you recycle all your glass and plastic containers, _____.

3 If you buy your computer online, _____.

4 If you review new vocabulary regularly, even when you don't have a test,

_____

5 If you carry an extra sweater in your backpack, _____.

6 If you read one book a month, _____.

Practice 16

Discuss these conditional sentences from "Eight Hours a Night" with a partner. Which ones use hedging? Underline the language that shows hedging. Which one doesn't use hedging? Why didn't the writer use hedging?

1 If students know that sleeping will have an effect on their final grade, they will surely take sleep more seriously.

2 If a school sets high expectations and rules about behavior, students will be more likely to work to reach those expectations.

3 If teachers show that they value rested students, it is probable that students will value their rest more, too.

C Punctuate conditionals

PUNCTUATING CONDITIONALS

Conditional sentences contain an *if*-clause and a main clause. When the *if*-clause comes first, it is followed by a comma.

If Mary has one more absence, the instructor may drop her from class.

When the main clause comes first, it is not followed by a comma.

The instructor may drop Mary from the class if she has one more absence.

Practice 17

Read a paragraph from a problem-solution essay. It contains five conditional sentences. Three of these contain errors of punctuation and three contain grammar errors (mistakes in verb tense). Find the mistakes and fix them.

> Second, if high school students will learn more about U.S. history they will likely be more active citizens when they are older. If they understand the events and trials that have led to universal suffrage, students value their right to vote. If they appreciate the historical development of voting rights in the United States it is possible that they will even feel honored by their right to vote. They will surely go to the polls and cast their vote. Voting is just the beginning of their participation as citizens, and it's an important step because it makes them feel a part of the political process. If they will feel that they are members of this process many of them will surely be inspired to participate even more. They will want to follow issues and get to know candidates if they realize that they are part of the decision-making process.

Your turn

Check your second draft. Examine the verb tenses and punctuation in any five conditionals you have used. Check for the strength and certainty of your predictions. Mark changes on your paper.

D Write the final draft

As you write your final draft, make the revisions and edits you have noted. Make sure that your spelling, punctuation, and formatting are correct and check for any grammar errors.

A Share your writing

> ### SMALL-GROUP READ-ALOUD
>
> In a Small-Group Read-Aloud, each person reads his or her essay or another student's essay out loud. Other group members listen, taking notes about especially interesting or unique ideas. After each person reads, the other group members make positive comments about the ideas in the essay, but do not comment on the grammar or organization.

Do a Small-Group Read-Aloud. Form a group of approximately four students. Read and comment on each other's compositions.

B Check your progress

After you get your essay back from your instructor, complete the *Progress Check* below.

PROGRESS CHECK

Date: _____

Essay title: _____

Things I did well in this essay:

_____

_____

_____

Things I need to work on in my next essay:

_____

_____

_____

Look at your *Progress Check* on page 39 of Chapter 1. How did you improve your writing in this essay?

_____

_____

_____

Comparison-Contrast Essays

How do you decide what product to buy or what job to apply for? You probably compare two or more different possibilities. You look at their similarities and differences to help you make the best choice.

In this chapter, you will write an essay pointing out similarities or differences between two things. You will state which you prefer and why. Perhaps your essay will convince the reader to make a similar choice.

A Think about the sample essay topic

You are going to read an essay comparing online friends and face-to-face friends. Before you read the essay, look at the information below about the most common online activities. Then discuss the questions below in a small group.

Figure 3.1 Activities of U.S. adults on the Internet, in millions per day

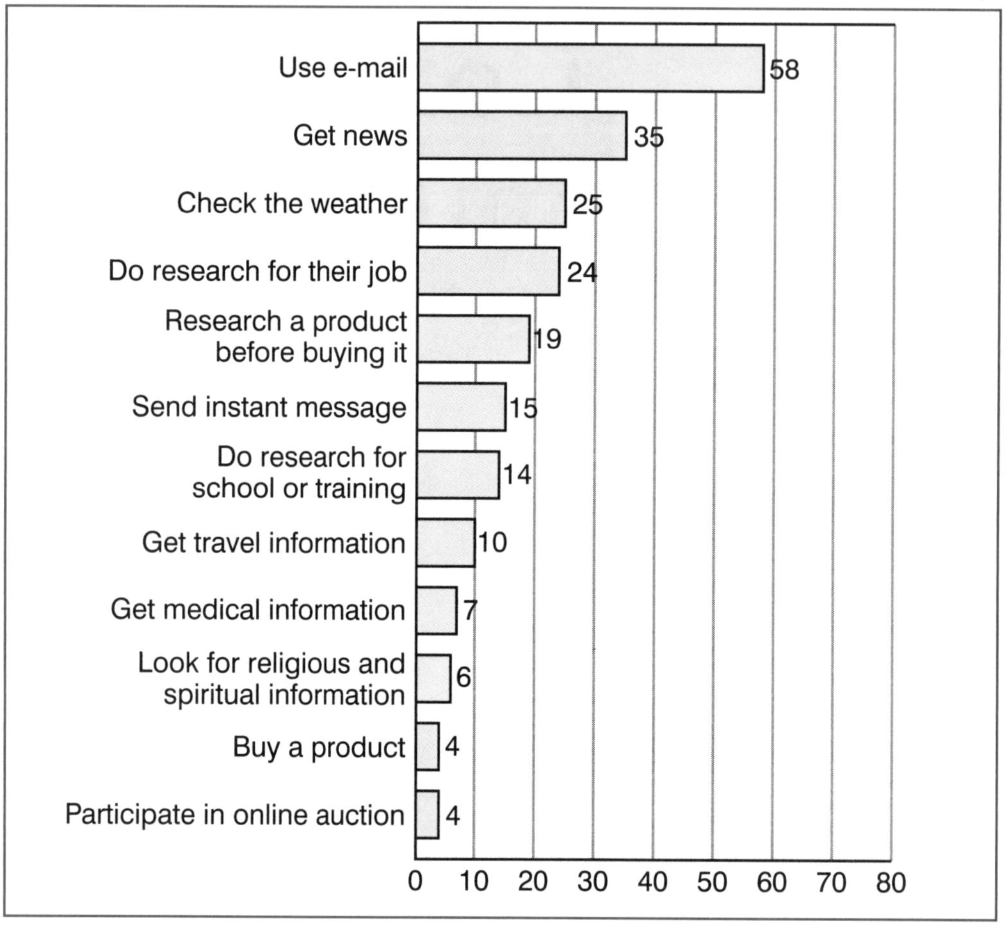

Source: Pew Internet & American Life Project Tracking, 2004

1 According to Figure 3.1, what are the most and least popular online activities?
2 Do people go online more for social reasons or for work or school? Why do you think this is true?
3 Did information in the chart surprise you? Why?
4 Which of the activities did you do yesterday? Within the last week? Which have you never done? How are you different from the average user shown in the chart?
5 What other things can people do online? Which of them have you done?
6 How much time do you spend each day communicating with friends online? In what ways do you communicate (for example, e-mail, instant messaging, etc.)?
7 Do you have online friends you have never met in person? Tell how you met them.

B Read the sample essay

As you read the essay, think about which kind of friend the writer prefers and why. Then share your ideas with a partner.

Friends.com

People have always needed friendship. Humans are very sociable creatures, so they need to interact with other people. Even if people have not changed much over the years, the way to make and enjoy friends has changed. These days, we can become friends with people we have never met by using the Internet. In fact, online friends have several advantages over face-to-face friends. You can communicate with online friends in new and different ways, you can share your feelings more deeply and honestly, and you can meet compatible friends that you would never have had the chance to know in the past.

The Internet offers special methods of communication. Traditionally, people talked with just one person face-to-face or on the phone, or to groups of people at parties or at school. On the other hand, only the Internet makes it possible to communicate with a large variety of different people sitting in different rooms all over the world. One example of this is the growing popularity of massive multiplayer online role-playing games, commonly called MMORPGs. In these online games, each player chooses a character and interacts with other players' characters. There can be 10 other players, or 50 or 100 or 1,000. Players can join and leave the game whenever they want to, and the next time they join the game, it will have changed depending on what other players did in that time. With traditional face-to-face friends, this would never be possible. You couldn't have players in South Korea, China, Australia, Germany, Canada, and other countries all playing the same game at the same time and talking to each other.

The feelings you have communicating online are special, too. When I am talking in person with a friend, I am more hesitant and shyer. I keep some of my ideas hidden. In contrast, when I am writing e-mails or IMing (instant messaging), I am more honest and open. Online communication feels safer and more confidential to me, and I don't fear people judging or criticizing me. I express my opinions more directly, and I share thoughts that I would never say out loud. I can't explain why this happens, but my friends tell me they feel the same way. I know when I receive e-mails and IMs, even from people I have never seen, they share more personal information than my face-to-face friends do. This kind of open and honest expression is a relief to me.

The most important advantage of online friends for me is the possibility of finding friends without any geographical restriction. No matter what country someone lives in, he or she can become a close friend. Because you are communicating more honestly and openly, you can make friends more quickly and easily, too. You can then decide to meet in person if you want to. In fact, I met my girlfriend online using MSN Messenger. I talked to her for many hours, and we shared some photos, so I got to know her very well. Then we met in person, and we have been dating since. If you can only

continued

meet friends in person, you can only meet people who live near you or go to school or work with you. Maybe you will like some of those people, but maybe you won't. If you don't like the people you see every day, you will have no friends. With the Internet, on the other hand, you can easily find friends who share your interests and opinions.

Both your face-to-face and your online friends are important. Unlike online friends, face-to-face friends can participate in sports with you or spend time with you even when you are not talking or communicating. Therefore, I am not suggesting that people should not have any face-to-face friends. However, if you want to try communicating in an exciting new way, if you want to share your feelings completely and honestly, or if you are looking for a compatible friend or partner, try looking online. When you turn on the computer, you are just a click away from meeting a whole new crowd of friends from all around the world.

Adapted from an essay by Miguel A. Caban Ruiz

C Notice the essay structure

COMPARISON-CONTRAST ESSAYS

A comparison-contrast essay usually either compares (examines similarities) or contrasts (examines differences). The writer first must have a reason for making a comparison or contrast; for example, to convince readers that one thing is better than another. The writer of "Friends.com" would have a rather boring essay if he just wrote that online friends and face-to-face friends have some similarities and differences. The reader already knows that. The reader wants to know, "Why are you writing this essay? What do you want me to believe or do?" There are several ways to convince your readers.

- **Compare:** Point out similarities between two seemingly different things.

    My teachers complain that students today spend more time online than they do reading. However, I think that using the computer benefits students in the same way that reading does.

- **Contrast:** Point out differences between two similar things.

    Even though video games and computer games seem similar in many ways, there are three important differences that explain why I prefer computer games.

- **Compare and contrast:** Occasionally, an essay may both compare and contrast, especially to explain two options that may be unfamiliar to readers.

    Before you can decide whether to buy a desktop or a laptop computer, you need to think about how you will use your computer. Desktops and laptops each have advantages and disadvantages that you should consider carefully before you make your choice.

Practice 1

Answer these questions about "Friends.com." Then discuss your answers with your classmates.

1 What is the thesis statement? Underline it <u>twice</u>.
2 Underline the topic sentence in each body paragraph.
3 Is the writer mostly comparing (showing similarities) or mostly contrasting (showing differences)?
4 What reason for preferring online friends to face-to-face friends did you find most convincing?
5 Were there any points you did not find convincing? If so, which ones and why?
6 What other reasons can you think of to support the writer's thesis statement?
7 What arguments can you think of that work against the writer's thesis statement?
8 In the conclusion, what action does the writer encourage readers to take?

D Select a topic

TOPICS

For a comparison-contrast essay, choose a topic about which people commonly express different opinions. After you choose your topic, think about the *purpose* for your essay. What do you want to convince your readers to do or think? For example, do you want to convince your readers to live in one place and not in another?

After you decide on your purpose, then decide whether you mainly want to compare or contrast. Remember that you will *compare* if you mainly want your readers to see the *similarities* between two things, and that you will *contrast* if you mainly want your readers to notice some important *differences*.

Practice 2

Read each topic and purpose for an essay. Circle whether the writer should mainly compare or mainly contrast. Discuss your ideas with a partner.

1 **Topic:** Deciding which airline to fly
   Purpose: To convince readers to just choose the least expensive one because airlines are basically the same
   a compare
   b contrast

2 **Topic:** Deciding which airline to fly
   Purpose: To explain how your choice will make the difference between a good trip and a bad one
   a compare
   b contrast

3 Topic: American English and British English

Purpose: To explain why native English speakers from different countries sometimes have trouble communicating

   a compare

   b contrast

4 Topic: American English and British English

Purpose: To show that it doesn't matter which variety of English you learn

   a compare

   b contrast

5 Topic: Study math in an online course or study in a traditional classroom

Purpose: To show that you can learn just as much either way

   a compare

   b contrast

6 Topic: Study math in an online course or study in a traditional classroom

Purpose: To persuade readers that you will learn math faster if you study online

   a compare

   b contrast

Your turn ↶

Choose a topic from the list below or use one of your own ideas. Then decide what your purpose is and whether you will compare or contrast.

1 Individual / team sports

2 Travel alone / with a tour group

3 Live near the city center / in the suburbs

4 Have a few close friends / many friends

5 Spend holidays with family / friends

6 Other topics: _____

> Topic: _____
>
> Purpose: _____
>
> I will mainly (circle one)
>
> **a** compare
>
> **b** contrast

E Brainstorm

VENN DIAGRAMS

Making a Venn diagram can help you organize your ideas as you brainstorm your topic. It also provides a way for you to see similarities and differences clearly. As you fill in your diagram with ideas, don't worry about whether you will use all the ideas in your essay. Just write as many ideas as you can.

Topic: American and British English

Purpose: To show that the differences between the two are not important to language learners

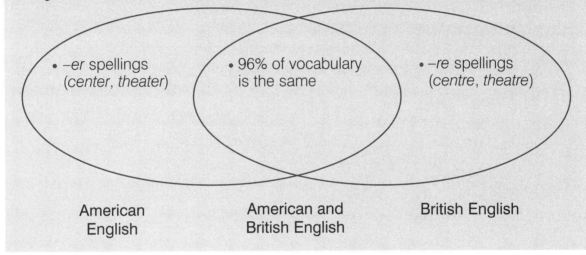

| American English | American and British English | British English |

Practice 3

Look at the list of ideas for "Friends.com." First, identify the topic and the purpose of the essay. Then write the ideas into the correct places in the Venn diagram on page 74. The first three ideas have been added for you.

more honest and open	express ideas and opinions
play sports, do activities in person	play MMORPG
communicate with one person at a time or in a small group	have to be in the same place
can live anywhere	can lie more easily
see facial expressions and body language	value both kinds
have to be awake at the same time	can spend time just being together, not communicating
play games	can communicate with large numbers of people at the same time
can meet people from anywhere (girlfriend)	

Topic: _____

Purpose: _____

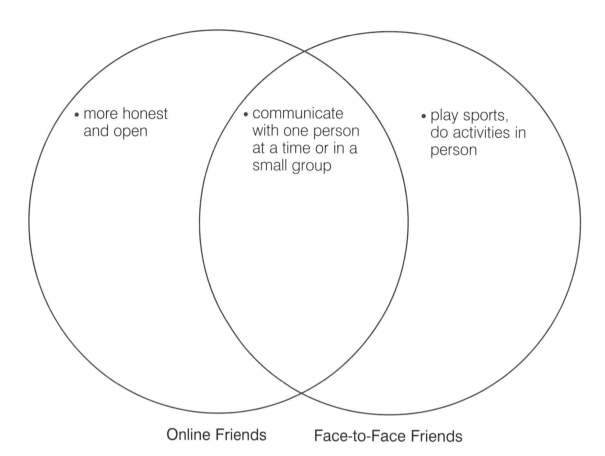

Online Friends   Face-to-Face Friends

Practice 4

Look at the Venn diagram in *Practice 3* and refer to the essay on pages 69-70. Which three ideas didn't the writer use for his essay? Mark those ideas with an *X*. Why do you think he didn't use those ideas? Discuss with a partner.

Your turn ↵

Brainstorm ideas for your topic and write them in a Venn diagram on a separate piece of paper.

F Discuss your ideas with others

With a partner or small group, take turns sharing your topics. Follow these steps.

1 Explain why you chose your topic, and what your purpose is. Say whether you plan to mainly compare or mainly contrast.

2 Explain the ideas in your Venn diagram. Say which ideas you will probably use in your essay.

3 If you get any more ideas while you are talking, or if your group members give you additional ideas, add them to your diagram.

A Compose the thesis statement

Write a thesis statement that includes your topic and your opinion.

B Edit your brainstorming

Look at your Venn diagram again and edit your brainstorming. Cross out any ideas that you don't like or that do not relate to your thesis statement. Check (✓) the ideas that you like the most. If you think of new ideas that are related to your thesis statement, add them now and revise your thesis statement.

C Add a sentence that shows scope

SHOWING THE SCOPE OF THE ESSAY

Often the thesis statement contains a preview of the main ideas that are going to be addressed in the essay. However, sometimes the thesis is expressed in more than one sentence. Additional sentences may preview, or show the scope of, the essay.

Look at the thesis from "Friends.com." The first sentence gives the topic and opinion while the second one shows scope. In this case, the second sentence previews for the reader the three main ideas that will be discussed in the body.

> In fact, online friends have several advantages over face-to-face friends. You can communicate with online friends in new and different ways, you can share your feelings more deeply and honestly, and you can meet compatible friends that you would never have had the chance to know in the past.

Practice 5

Look back at the sample essays in Chapter 1 (pages 15-16) and Chapter 2 (pages 43-44). Is there a preview of the scope? If so, which sentence is it?

Your turn 〰

Write your thesis statement with a sentence that shows the scope of your essay.

D Organize your essay

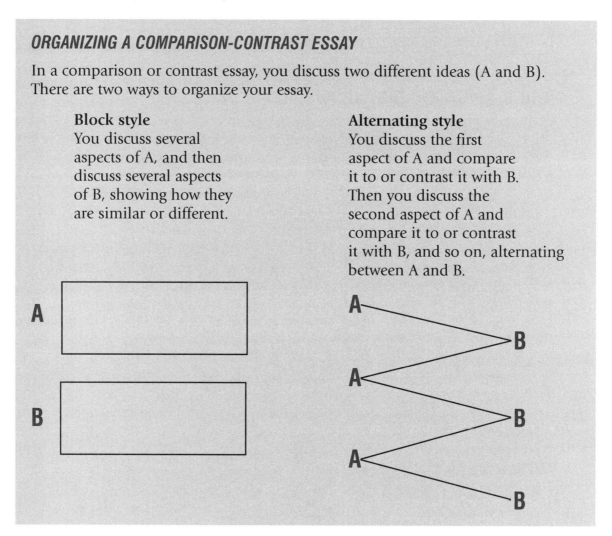

ORGANIZING A COMPARISON-CONTRAST ESSAY

In a comparison or contrast essay, you discuss two different ideas (A and B). There are two ways to organize your essay.

Block style
You discuss several aspects of A, and then discuss several aspects of B, showing how they are similar or different.

Alternating style
You discuss the first aspect of A and compare it to or contrast it with B. Then you discuss the second aspect of A and compare it to or contrast it with B, and so on, alternating between A and B.

Practice 6

Look at some brainstorming notes, in Venn diagram form on the next page, for an essay comparing reading books (A) to reading online (B). Then read the two different body paragraphs that follow. In which one does the writer use block-style organization? In which does she use alternating-style organization? Which paragraph do you prefer? Explain your answers to a partner.

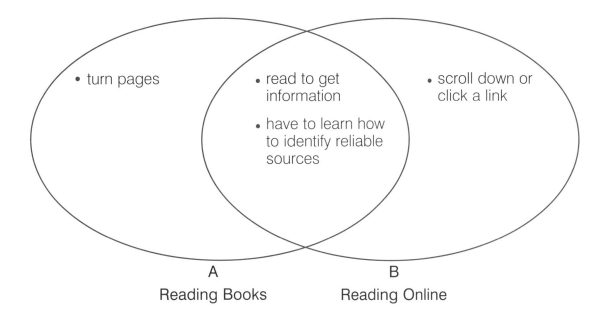

A
Reading Books

B
Reading Online

1   Whether you turn the physical page of a book from, say, page 26 to 27, or click a link that says "next," reading a book and reading online involve similar skills. You are still reading to find information, which means that you have to understand what you have read so that you can restate it in your own words. There are millions of books and journals; similarly, there are millions of Web pages, so no matter what your topic is, you will need to use your judgment to determine whether the author is a qualified expert on the topic and whether the information is recent.

2   Some teachers worry that their students who research online are losing valuable reading skills. Traditionally, students would go to the library to look for information. They had to look through many books, magazines, and journals to find ones that were relevant to their topic and that were quality sources. As they read their books, the students had to process the information to understand it. In the same way, students who research online look through many different Web sites to find the relevant ones. They also have to judge the reliability of each site. Even though they scroll or click from page to page instead of turning over a piece of paper, the process of reading is the same.

Practice 7

Analyze the organization in the second body paragraph in "Friends.com." Follow these steps. Use the example on page 78 as a guide on how to mark up the paragraphs.

1 Label with an A the sentences that describe face-to-face friends.
2 Label with a B the sentences that describe online friends.
3 Draw vertical lines to show where the writer changes from A to B.
4 Underline the phrase the writer uses to show that he is changing.
5 Say which type of organization the writer is following: block style or alternating style.

A = Studying English in own country
B = Studying English in the United States

[A] If you study English in your own country, all of your classmates will speak your native language. [A] They will make the same language mistakes that you do. [A] Usually you talk to them in your native language, because it is so easy. | [B] In contrast, if you study English in the U.S., your classmates will probably come from many different countries. [B] They . . .

Organization: *block*

Your turn ↷

Decide which type of organization you are going to use for your essay.

E Make an outline

Make an outline for your essay similar to the one on the right. Complete it by writing key words, phrases, and ideas. Add support for each main idea.

I. INTRODUCTION
Hook
Thesis statement
Sentence that shows the scope
II. FIRST MAIN IDEA
Support
III. SECOND MAIN IDEA
Support
IV. THIRD MAIN IDEA
Support
V. CONCLUSION

Practice 8

With a partner or in a small group, share your outline and discuss the order of your main ideas. Follow these steps.

1 Show your outline to your partner or classmates. Discuss the topic. Is it clear? Is it interesting?
2 Discuss the main idea in each body paragraph. Discuss the explanations for each main point. Are they clear?
3 Discuss the order of the paragraphs. Is it the most effective order?

F Use language for comparing and contrasting

> ## LANGUAGE FOR COMPARING AND CONTRASTING
>
> Here are some useful words for pointing out similarities:
>
> A . . . *In the same way*, B . . .
> A . . . *Similarly*, B . . .
> *Like* A . . . , B . . .
> *Both* A *and* B . . .
> *Neither* A . . . *nor* B . . .
>
> Face-to-face friends enjoy talking together. <u>In the same way</u> / <u>Similarly</u>, online friends value dialogues.
>
> <u>Neither</u> face-to-face friends <u>nor</u> online friends have to be the same age.
>
> Here are some useful words for pointing out differences:
>
> A . . . *On the other hand*, B . . .
> A . . . *In contrast*, B . . .
> *Unlike* A . . . , B . . .
> *While* A . . . , B . . .
>
> Face-to-face friends can use body language to communicate. <u>On the other hand</u> / <u>In contrast</u>, online friends must rely on written words.
>
> <u>Unlike</u> face-to-face friends, who can use body language to communicate, online friends must rely on written words.

Practice 9

Reread "Friends.com." Circle words and phrases that show comparison and contrast. Compare your results with a partner.

Practice 10

Circle the correct transition word or phrase.

1 *Like / Unlike* modern food, traditional food was eaten close to the place where it had been grown.

2 Teenagers today spend time relaxing with computer games and surfing the Internet. *Similarly / On the other hand*, people from my parents' generation relaxed by watching television.

3 *Both / Neither* team sports *and / nor* individual sports increase strength and give us feelings of enjoyment and accomplishment.

4 When you play on a team, every member contributes to its success or failure. *In the same way / On the other hand*, when you play an individual sport, the responsibility and the reward are yours alone.

5 *While / Unlike* using public transportation saves money and fuel, it takes more time for most people.

6 *Like / Unlike* traveling with a tour guide, traveling alone helps you mature and learn to face challenges on your own.

7 *Both / Neither* telephone calls *and / nor* e-mails are as personal as face-to-face communication.

8 *Like / Unlike* a good friend, a brother or sister knows you well and accepts both your good points and bad points.

9 When you watch a movie, you can see what the characters look like and hear their voices. *Similarly / In contrast*, when you read a book, you create these details in your own mind.

Practice 11

Connect the sentences with appropriate language. Then share your sentences with a partner. Did you connect them in the same way?

1 If you live at home while you attend college, you don't have to worry about housework and cooking. If you live by yourself in an apartment, you will have to take care of your home as well as your homework.

2 Online friends don't know everything about you. Face–to-face friends only know the information you choose to share with them.

3 When you read a book, you move from one page sequentially to the next page. When you read online, you can move from one page to many different pages just by clicking on different links.

4 When you write with pen and paper, you can easily cross out ideas you don't like and add new ideas. When you use a computer, you can delete ideas you don't want to use and type new information.

Your turn

Write your body paragraphs. For each of your body paragraphs, use a transition to show when you are moving from A to B.

G Write the first draft

In this section, you have written your thesis statement, a sentence showing the scope of your essay, and the body paragraphs with transition words. Now put together your first draft by adding the following:

- an introduction with a hook and background information
- a conclusion that summarizes your main points and either makes a prediction or offers a closing thought
- a title

A Benefit from peer feedback

Exchange essays and books with a partner. Fill out the form below about your partner's essay. Then return the book and discuss your answers.

PEER FEEDBACK FORM

Writer's name: _____   Date: _____

Reviewer's name: _____

1 On your partner's paper, underline the thesis statement <u>twice</u>.

2 Answer these questions about the introduction. Mark each ✓ or X .

   ☐ Does the introductory paragraph have an interesting hook?
   ☐ Is the topic clear?
   ☐ Does the thesis statement tell you the writer's opinion?
   ☐ Is there a sentence that shows the scope?

3 Does the essay mainly compare, mainly contrast, or compare and contrast?

   _____

4 Underline the topic sentence of each body paragraph.

5 Did the writer use block style or alternating style organization?

   _____

6 Find and circle words or expressions that compare or contrast. How many did

   the writer use? _____

7 Answer these questions about the conclusion. Mark each ✓ or X .

   ☐ Does the conclusion summarize the writer's main points?
   ☐ Does the conclusion include any new main points?
   ☐ Does the conclusion refer back to the hook?

8 Draw a star (★) in the margin next to your two or three favorite sentences.
   Put a question mark (?) next to any sentences that you did not understand.

9 Look for transitions such as FANBOYS, *in addition, however, because,* and
   therefore. Circle them. How many of these transitions did the writer use? ____

10 Any other comments: _____

   _____

   _____

B Connecting paragraphs

CONNECTING PARAGRAPHS TO THE INTRODUCTION

In the introduction, a sentence showing scope gives a preview of the main points that will be discussed in the body of the essay. In the body, each topic sentence then connects back to this sentence by referring to one of the ideas contained in the preview sentence.

Notice, for example, how each of the topic sentences in the essay "Friends.com" connects back to the preview sentence at the end of the introduction.

Preview sentence	Topic sentences
You can communicate with online friends in new and different ways, you can share your feelings more deeply and honestly, and you can meet compatible friends that you would never have had the chance to know in the past.	The Internet offers special methods of communication. The feelings you have communicating online are special, too. The most important advantage of online friends for me is the possibility to find friends without any geographical restriction.

Writers can use transitions like the ones below to connect paragraphs back to the introduction and to help the reader know his or her place in the essay. However, using these transitions for every paragraph can make your essay seem too simplistic, so only use them for one or two body paragraphs, rather than in every one.

The first similarity is . . . A second similarity is . . . Finally, . . .	Another important consideration is . . . A second major advantage is . . . The final reason is . . .

Practice 12

Read the thesis statement below. Underline the parts that show the scope of the essay. With a partner, write a topic sentence for each of the body paragraphs. Then compare your topic sentences with another pair of students.

> . . . American and British English have different spellings, different grammar, and different idioms.

1 _____

2 _____

3 _____

Your turn ↝

Look at your body paragraphs. Do the topic sentences connect back to a preview sentence in the introduction? Add any transitions that make your essay clearer.

C Critical thinking

Practice 13

In each of the following paragraphs, cross out any sentence that is not relevant.

1   Furthermore, a laptop computer is more convenient than a desktop. A desktop computer stays in one place, on your desk at work or at home. In contrast, you can carry a laptop with you when you go to work or school. You might need to buy a carrying case, though. You can also bring it with you when you travel. These days, it's easy to find Internet cafés in every city, so that's also very convenient.

2   In addition to having different vocabulary and grammar, British and American English use different idioms and expressions. These can cause communication problems. For example, last summer I worked in an office in London. It took me a long time to get used to the British accents. Once, I accidentally deleted a document from my manager's computer. I never did anything like that again, though. He said, "That's a bit of a nuisance." Because "a bit of" means "a very small amount" to an American, I thought he wasn't very upset, so I didn't apologize. However, a British person would have known that "a bit of a" problem was actually serious, and I should have apologized and tried to fix the problem.

3   Some people say another reason to fly in business class is that the seats are more comfortable. Is it really worth hundreds of dollars just to sit in a softer seat for three hours? Usually I just sleep on the airplane or watch the movie anyway. It doesn't matter how wide or soft the seat is if I am asleep or concentrating on something else. However, I don't like it when I get on a plane and the movie is something I've just seen recently. Then I prefer to read a book. I once got upgraded to a business class seat on a flight. I admit that the seat was a little nicer, but the difference in seat quality was just not big enough to justify the difference in price.

D Make revision decisions

Reread your essay and think about the peer feedback from your partner. Check your paper for irrelevant sentences and mark any other changes that you want to make.

E Write the second draft

Use the notes you wrote on your first draft to make revisions. Write the second draft.

A Use academic language

> ### ACADEMIC LANGUAGE
>
> Written language is more formal than spoken language, and academic writing is more formal than, for example, friendly letters or e-mails. Some features of academic writing are:
>
> - It does not use unconventional spellings and abbreviations.
>   - X The government is gonna increase taxes.
>   - ✓ The government is going to increase taxes.
>   - X The law was passed on Dec. 12.
>   - ✓ The law was passed on December 12.
> - It avoids casual language and slang expressions.
>   - X Students were, like, really surprised by the test.
>   - ✓ Students were surprised by the test.
>   - X A new research facility would require a lot of dough.
>   - ✓ A new research facility would require a lot of money.

Practice **14**

Change the underlined words and phrases to sound more academic. Then compare your new paragraph with a partner's paragraph.

> Most students of English know some of the common differences in <u>vocab</u> between American and British English. Americans ride an elevator, but <u>Brits</u> use a lift. Americans live in an apartment, while British people live in a flat. However, those differences aren't <u>really a big deal</u>. Ninety-six percent of the vocabulary in American and British English is the same, so there are <u>way more</u> similarities than differences. <u>What's more</u>, because of <u>TV</u>, books, movies, <u>etc.</u>, most people already know the common differences. Even if they read an unfamiliar word, <u>I bet</u> they can guess its meaning from the context. Students should think of the differences as <u>cool</u> and not <u>get stressed out</u> by them.

Your turn ↩

Check the language in your essay. Are there words or phrases that are too informal? If you are not sure how to correct them, check a dictionary or ask your instructor.

B Use comparative structures

COMPARING ADJECTIVES AND ADVERBS

Whether you are comparing or contrasting, you will often use comparative forms of adjectives, or comparative structures with nouns. Consider these examples.

Reading an article online is <u>slower than</u> reading a printed article.

Reading an article online takes <u>more time than</u> reading a printed article.

Count the syllables in the adjective you want to use. Then follow these rules to form the comparative:

- Adjectives and adverbs of one syllable: Add *–er* to the end.

 small → smaller (than)
 fast → faster (than)

- Adjectives of two syllables that end in *–y*: Drop the *–y* and add *–ier*.

 funny → funnier (than)
 happy → happier (than)

- Adverbs of two syllables that end in *–y*: Use with *more . . . than.*

 quickly → more quickly (than)
 safely → more safely (than)

- Adjectives and adverbs of two or more syllables: Use with *more . . . than.*

 complicated → more complicated (than)
 happily → more happily (than)

There are a few common exceptions to these rules:

 good → better (than)
 bad → worse (than)
 fun → more fun (than)

Practice 15

Go back to "Friends.com" on pages 69-70. Circle all of the comparative adjectives and adverbs you find. Share your results with a partner. Did you find all of them?

INTENSIFYING COMPARISONS

To make comparisons stronger, add a modifier before the *–er* form of the adjective or before the word *more.* The expressions below are ranked in order of increasing strength:

somewhat stronger	somewhat more complicated
considerably stronger	considerably more complicated
much / far stronger	much / far more complicated
significantly stronger	significantly more complicated

Practice 16

Read the paragraph. Underline the mistakes with comparatives. Edit the paragraph to fix the mistakes.

> Business class is more significantly comfortable as economy class. First of all, the seats are more wide and more soft. I can stretch out my legs easier because of the extra space. A second advantage is that the food is far more delicious. The meals are more fresh in business class than in economy class, and they're prepared better, too. The movies that are shown in business class are more recently and more popular. Even the flight attendants are somewhat friendlier to customers in business class. They speak politer and give good service. Even if it considerably costs more money, I will always fly business class.

Your turn ✐

Check your essay for correct use of comparative adjectives and adverbs. Add intensifiers to your comparatives where appropriate. Correct any errors.

C Write the final draft

As you write your final draft, make the revisions and edits you have noted. Make sure that your spelling, punctuation, and formatting are correct, and check for any grammar errors.

V FOLLOWING UP

A Share your writing

Work in a small group. Take turns and follow these steps.

1 Tell your group about the two things you compared or contrasted. Then ask your group to brainstorm some similarities and differences. Finally, ask them to say which one they prefer.
2 Read your essay aloud, or let each member of your group read a copy.
3 What did your group think of your essay? Did your essay change anyone's mind? Did it strengthen ideas they already held?

B Check your progress

After you get your essay back from your instructor, complete the *Progress Check* below.

PROGRESS CHECK

Date: _____

Essay title: _____

Things I did well in this essay:

_____

_____

_____

Things I need to work on in my next essay:

_____

_____

_____

Look back at your *Progress Check* from Chapter 2 on page 65. How did you improve your writing in this essay?

_____

_____

_____

Persuasive Essays

What controversial topics do you discuss with your friends and classmates? Do you examine all sides of an issue before you take a position? Are you often able to convince your friends of your opinion?

In this chapter, you will write a persuasive essay. You will learn how to present and support your arguments, how to counter likely opposing arguments, and how to convince your reader of your point of view.

A Think about the sample essay topic

You are going to read an essay by a student who is concerned because many women are choosing to have fewer children in her country. The student's essay is controversial because she argues for changes that would transform Japanese society. Before you read the essay, look at the information in the graph and discuss the questions that follow.

Figure 4.1 Fertility rate changes in selected countries

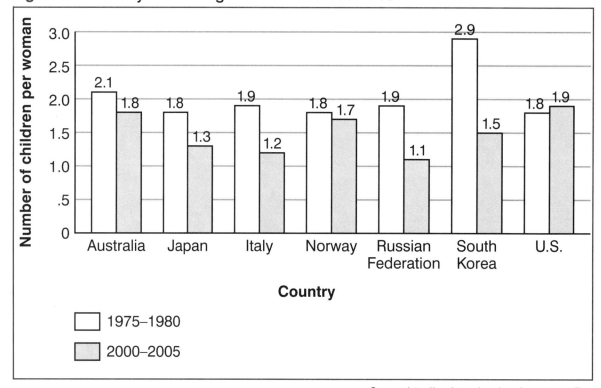

Source: http://earthtrends.wri.org/country_profiles

1 Why do you think people are having fewer babies in some countries?

2 What happens to a country when its birthrate declines? What might be some benefits and drawbacks in this situation?

3 Do you plan on having children? Do you plan on having a career? Why is it difficult to do both?

4 Should companies and governments help working couples care for their children? If so, what should they do? If not, why not? How would you persuade someone of your point of view?

B Read the sample essay

You are going to read an essay on shrinking families in Japan. As you read the essay, ask yourself what the writer's main point is and whether the writer has persuaded you to adopt her point of view. Then share your ideas with a partner.

Bringing Babies Back to Japan

Japanese society is facing its most serious threat in recent years. Japan's birthrate keeps falling steadily. If this continues, the population will get smaller and smaller. While the number of babies is decreasing, the average Japanese life span is increasing. It is one of the longest in the world. This is a national catastrophe because there are fewer working-age people who pay into the social security system, and there will eventually be too few workers. The Japanese can no longer delay addressing the issue of its shrinking population. The only way to grow the population is by bringing babies back to Japan. Japan's entire social structure, including families, businesses, and the government, must work together to encourage families to have babies.

In the past, many people thought raising children to be the only goal and responsibility of women. Now, Japanese women no longer seem interested solely in raising children, and society needs to accept this. Japanese women want to work, either for money or for their own interests. In fact, like many women in the world today, they would like to both work and raise children. But Japanese society is against this. Some companies, for example, even tell women to quit working when they get married or have children. As a result, Japanese women are having fewer children or no children at all. Society should help set up ways for them both to work and to have children.

One major force in society that has the power to enable women both to work and to raise children is Japanese companies. Usually, people don't think of a company as a force in shaping families, but this attitude should be reconsidered. Japanese companies need to recognize their role in shaping families and think more about supporting them. First, they should offer affordable child care, and the government should help them. This would allow women to have children and still have a good career. According to my pen pal in Norway, for example, Norway has a good system of child care, where working mothers can even visit their children at lunchtime. Furthermore, in Norway, you can see a high rate of working women and a stable birthrate. The Norwegian child-care system is an appropriate example for Japan to follow.

Even though the raising of children is not an easy job or a traditional job for Japanese men, we must accept that it is partly men's work, too. It is essential that Japanese fathers help more in the home. After all, the children are theirs, too. Also, the Japanese government and companies should set up a better system of parental leave so that both parents can care for their families. My brother-in-law, for example, didn't take his parental leave because he thought it would hurt his career. I have heard many similar stories. It is important that fathers be able to take parental leave without threatening their jobs. In Norway, for instance, men can and do

continued

take paternity leave without concern for their careers. Perhaps Japanese companies should consider making paternity leave a requirement so that there could be no question about its impact on one's career. Paternity leave is important because it helps families to understand the father's role sooner, when babies are young.

Some Japanese couples think that parenting is too expensive. It is a pity that couples have to abandon having children for economic reasons. It is the government's job to help make child raising more affordable. Many countries' governments are using different ways to help parents financially. These may include tax breaks or one-time payments to new parents. While it is true that many people don't want to pay higher taxes to support other people's children, producing the next generation of Japan is a question of our nation's existence. Everyone, therefore, must help pay.

Increasing the birthrate is a key defense against the shrinking of Japanese society. There needs to be a balance between raising children and working. In order to find this balance, all members of Japanese society should participate in raising and paying for the cost of children. In the long run, a vibrant young population helps everyone, including companies, families, and taxpayers, in Japanese society. We had better take matters seriously for a bright Japanese future. Imagine your own old age, without any children. What would happen?

Adapted from an essay by Yuki Nagami

C Notice the essay structure

ORGANIZATION OF PERSUASIVE ESSAYS

A persuasive essay is like an imaginary dialogue between a reader and the writer. The writer uses arguments to try to convince the reader to think something or to take a certain action. But the writer also has to imagine how the reader will argue against his or her arguments, and answer those objections.

Body paragraphs in persuasive essays, therefore, often have a unique organization. First the writer expresses a reader's likely response (a counterargument) to the argument that will follow. Then the writer presents the argument and its support. By addressing a reader's likely response first, the writer strengthens his position.

The organization of such a body paragraph looks like this:

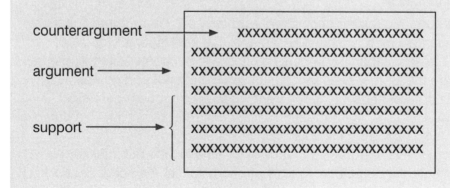

Practice 1

Answer these questions about "Bringing Babies Back to Japan." Then discuss your answers with your classmates.

1 What is the thesis statement? Underline it <u>twice</u>.

2 This essay has four body paragraphs. Underline the topic sentence in each one.

3 Look at the following lists. They show the four main arguments and the four counterarguments in the essay. Draw lines to match the counterarguments with the arguments.

Counterarguments	Arguments
Looking after children is hard work, and most Japanese men don't have experience with it.	Japanese companies need to make it easy for working parents to keep their jobs and have children, too.
Nobody wants to pay for another person's children.	Women should be able to have a career and to raise children.
Many people consider child raising the work of women.	Men must also participate in raising children.
It is not generally considered a company's job to help raise families.	Producing Japan's next generation is so important that the nation should offer attractive financial incentive for this work.

4 Find where the four arguments and counterarguments appear in the essay. Notice that in one paragraph the counterargument does not come at the beginning of the paragraph. Which paragraph is it?

5 Which of the following functions does the conclusion serve? Check (✓) as many as apply.

_____ It summarizes the arguments.

_____ It recommends a course of action.

_____ It gives a final comment on the topic.

6 If you were writing on this topic, what other arguments would you use to support the writer's thesis?

D Select a topic

CHOOSING A TOPIC

When you select a topic for a persuasive essay, choose one that is controversial. It should not be a topic about which most people have the same opinion. You should also choose a topic that you have a strong opinion about. It should be a topic that you have some personal connection to and that you know something about.

Here are some good questions to ask yourself as you choose your topic:

1 Is this really a controversial topic that people will have different opinions about?
2 Do I have a strong opinion about this topic?
3 Do I have enough knowledge about this topic?
4 Do I have a personal connection to this topic?
5 Will my readers be interested in this topic?

Practice 2

The writer of "Bringing Babies Back to Japan" brainstormed about her topic before she chose it for her essay. Read her brainstorm notes below. They show why this is a good topic for this writer because the content of each underlined part shows that she could have answered "yes" to the five questions in the *Choosing a Topic* box. Discuss with a partner how each underlined part matches up with one of the questions in the box.

My sister wants to have two kids. She's an architect and she wants to keep her paid job. Child care is so expensive, they can't afford it. Lots of couples can't afford it. It makes me angry. My sister is 37 and still has no children. This is sad because she really wants kids. Her husband can't help because of his company's rules. My friends and their families have the same problem. My pen pal in Norway says it's easier there. They have great ideas. Companies offer affordable daycare. Government gives tax incentives there. Men take leave to help raise children.

Japanese culture doesn't train men to help with raising children. It's a huge problem. I know not everyone will agree with me, but everybody needs to work together to solve this problem. Someday I want to have children, but I don't want to have to give up my career to do it. I'm not the only one. This affects everybody.

Your turn ⁀

Choose a topic from the list below or use one of your own ideas. Ask yourself the questions in the box *Choosing a Topic* on page 94.

1 The adoption of children from a foreign country

2 Cell phone manners or safety

3 Requirements for getting into a university

4 Global warming

5 Downloading music or movies without paying

6 School uniforms

7 Other topic: _____

E Brainstorm arguments

Follow these steps to find arguments to support your topic.

1 Brainstorm about your topic using listing or freewriting.

2 Read through your brainstorming notes and circle any arguments that you can use to support your topic.

3 Write down three arguments that you might use in your essay.

F Discuss your ideas with others

With a partner or in a small group, follow these steps to share your topic and your main arguments.

1 Explain why you chose your topic.

2 Ask your classmates if the topic is interesting to them.

3 Explain to your classmates your main arguments. Ask them which arguments they think are the most persuasive.

4 Ask what other arguments they can think of to support your thesis.

5 Ask what arguments they can think of that oppose your thesis.

6 Choose three or four arguments to focus on in your essay. Write them down.

A Compose the thesis statement

> ### *PERSUASIVE ESSAY THESIS STATEMENTS*
>
> An effective thesis statement for a persuasive essay contains the following:
> - the topic
> - the writer's opinion about the topic
> - a course of action, either implied or stated
> - the reason the course of action is necessary

Practice 3

In each pair of sentences, decide which sentence is not an effective thesis statement for a persuasive essay and explain why. Then identify the elements that make the other sentence an effective thesis statement.

1 a Private gun ownership should be legal because it increases the safety of individual citizens.

  b Private gun ownership is a hot topic of debate among Americans.

2 a Teachers who grade students strictly inspire their students to perform at a higher level.

  b Teachers in the United States don't grade as strictly as teachers in my country.

3 a Recent technological innovations have made battery-operated cars more fuel-efficient.

  b Governments should increase buyers' motivation to purchase battery-operated cars because of their fuel efficiency.

4 a To prevent people from taking drugs, we need to first understand why they are tempted by drugs.

  b People who take drugs are often aware of the dangers of drug use, but they abuse them anyway.

5 a Following a traditional Greek diet can help you lose weight and build health.

  b Greeks eat a lot of olives and olive oil, which are high in "good fat."

6 a High schools should help students find part-time jobs in their field of interest, both to help them learn the employment process and to gain work experience.

  b High schools don't support students' career building enough.

Your turn ✐

Write the thesis statement for your essay.

B Plan the introduction

CATCHY HOOKS

Remember that you should begin an essay with something that catches your reader's interest – a hook. Review some common hooks in the box *Hooks* on page 29. Then look at three other ways to help you get ideas for your hook.

- Appeal to emotions or find multiple meanings in key words in your title or thesis.

    Babies are so sweet and adorable and lovely. But what if women stopped wanting them?

- Put forward a common stereotype that you might challenge in your essay.

    All women want to do is to stay home and bring up babies. Right? Wrong!

- Refer to a song, a common saying, or proverb that relates to your topic.

    A famous Japanese poem compares the treasure of children to silver, gold, and jewels. But many Japanese women are saying, "No children for me!"

Your turn ∿

Write down three or four possible hooks for your introduction. Show them to a partner. Have your partner tell you which hook might work best for your topic.

C Organize your arguments

IDENTIFYING THE STRONGEST ARGUMENTS

The main ideas in a persuasive essay should be ordered to maximize their persuasiveness. It is often a good idea to put your strongest argument at the end. That way your reader considers it last and may finish your essay feeling persuaded.

Identifying your strongest argument often requires thinking and rethinking the possibilities. Consider which arguments are most persuasive, and also which ones you can most easily support with explanations, examples, and facts.

Follow these steps to help you decide the best order for the arguments in your persuasive essay.

1 Write your three or four main arguments each on a separate slip of paper.
2 Put the slips on your desk in any order. Read through them.
3 Put the arguments in emphatic order. (See the box *Emphatic Order* on page 23.)
4 Now mix up the slips of paper and exchange them with a partner.
5 Put your partner's arguments in emphatic order while your partner orders yours.
6 Discuss the orders you chose. If your partner ordered your arguments differently, talk about why. However, the final decision will be yours.

D Add counterarguments

DOUBLE LISTS

A persuasive essay tries to convince the readers to think or to believe something or to take a certain action. Therefore, when you write a persuasive essay, it is important to consider your audience. Who are your readers and what are their likely opinions about your topic? Once you identify the likely arguments against your topic, you can counter them more effectively.

To help you identify your reader's counterarguments, try making a *double list*. On one side put your arguments, and on the other the counterarguments you anticipate from your readers. Even if you will not write directly about these counterarguments against your topic, you should know what they are so that you can think of ways to make your own arguments stronger.

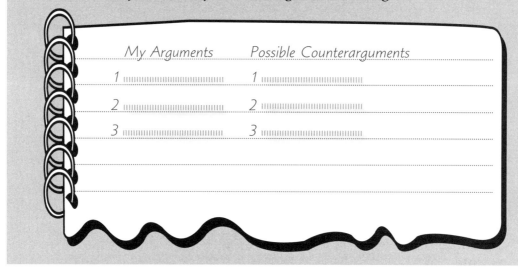

Practice 4

Here is a double list of ideas a writer made for his argument: *Fast food is bad for you*. Complete the chart on the following page by writing the ideas into either the "Arguments against" or the "Arguments for" column (three ideas have already been placed for you). Then draw a line to show which argument for the writer's opinion responds to an argument that is against the writer's opinion.

most fast food is very high in calories	salt raises blood pressure
can cause expensive medical problems	salty food tastes good
convenient	easy to eat too often
most fast-food places offer salads as a choice	cheap

Essay title: Fast Food Is Bad for You

Arguments against my opinion	Arguments for my opinion
• most fast-food places offer salads as a choice	• can cause expensive medical problems
•	• most fast food is very high in calories
•	•
•	•

Your turn ↻

Follow these steps to develop your arguments.

1 Write down your topic and four arguments that you might use in your persuasive essay. Write each argument on a different piece of paper.

2 Give the four pieces of paper to four different classmates and have each person write a counterargument to it.

3 When you get the pieces of paper back, make a double list of your arguments and counterarguments.

E Use argumentative language

LANGUAGE FOR INTRODUCING COUNTERARGUMENTS

When writing a persuasive essay, writers often present the counterargument first and then their own argument. You can introduce the counterargument and argument with phrases such as the following:

Counterargument	Argument
Some people believe . . .	However, it must also be recognized that . . .
While it is true that . . . ,	it can also be argued that . . .
Although many people claim that . . . ,	one can also argue that . . .

Practice 5

Read the arguments and counterarguments. Then write one or two sentences that introduce them. The first one has been done for you as an example.

1 Counterargument: Most fast-food places offer salads as a choice.
Argument: Most fast food is very high in calories.

While it is true that most fast-food places offer salads as a choice, it must also be recognized that most fast food is very high in calories.

2 Counterargument: Riding the bus can save money.
Argument: Time is money, and taking the bus usually takes much longer.

3 Counterargument: Private gun ownership keeps us safe because guns may deter criminals from entering homes.
Argument: Guns are too dangerous for private citizens to keep in their homes because of the possibility of accidents.

4 Counterargument: Plastic is bad for the environment.
Argument: Some newer plastics are readily biodegradable.

5 Counterargument: Change can be very difficult and stressful.
Argument: If we don't make changes in our lives, our lives would be very boring.

6 Counterargument: Studying overseas is expensive.
Argument: Studying overseas gives invaluable exposure to another culture.

Your turn

Look at the double list that you made in the *Your Turn* following *Practice 4* on page 99. Write sentences that introduce the counterarguments and the arguments. Some of these sentences may serve as good topic sentences in your body paragraphs.

F Choose support

TYPES OF SUPPORT

Writers use different types of support to argue or prove their points. The type of support a writer uses will depend on the topic, the audience, and the assignment. Of course, writers can use more than one kind of support in an essay.

- **Personal experience:** The writer tells about an experience he or she has had.
- **Expert opinion:** The writer tells another person's opinion. The other person should know a lot about the topic or have some personal experience that is relevant.
- **Examples:** The writer describes an instance of something to illustrate the point.
- **Analogy:** The writer compares the situation to another similar situation.
- **Facts and statistics:** The writer uses true statements or numbers to prove the idea. Often this information comes from other sources, such as books, newspapers, or Web sites.
- **Reason:** The writer uses reasoning or logic to argue the point.
- **Emotion:** The writer makes an emotional appeal to the reader.

Practice 6

What types of support are used in the following sentences? Write the letter of the kind of support next to each of the sentences below. The first one has been done for you.

a personal experience	**d** analogy	**f** reason
b expert opinion	**e** facts and statistics	**g** emotion
c examples		

_a_ 1 I once spent three hours researching a basic fact on the Internet.

____ 2 Driving cars hurts the planet in the same way that smoking cigarettes hurts the body.

____ 3 Individual citizens cannot always understand the impact of their actions. Therefore, the government has the responsibility to make laws to protect the environment from individuals.

____ 4 The geophysicist M. King Hubbert says, "Our ignorance is not so vast as our failure to use what we know."

____ 5 When employers offer their overweight employees a cash bonus to lose weight, those workers lose an average of 10 to 15 pounds.

____ 6 Managing the demand for transportation can provide multiple benefits, such as less traffic, increased safety, and improved environmental quality.

____ 7 It would be a great tragedy indeed to allow this situation to continue.

G Make a detailed outline

Follow these steps to complete a detailed outline for your persuasive essay.

1 Make an outline similar to the one on the right.
2 Write your hook.
3 Note any background information you need to include.
4 Write your thesis statement.
5 List the arguments that you will use in the body paragraphs of your essay.
6 For each argument, write two or three specific pieces of support. Include different types of support, such as reason, personal example, expert opinion, and so on.
7 Plan your conclusion.

I. INTRODUCTION
    Hook
    Background
    Thesis statement

II. FIRST MAIN IDEA
    Support 1
    Support 2
    Support 3

III. SECOND MAIN IDEA
    Support 1
    Support 2
    Support 3

IV. THIRD MAIN IDEA
    Support 1
    Support 2
    Support 3

V. CONCLUSION

H Write the first draft

In this section, you have planned all the pieces that you need for your essay. You have thought through the major arguments, counterarguments, and support for your essay. You have also considered the introduction and the conclusion. Put these pieces together to create the first draft of your essay. Add a title.

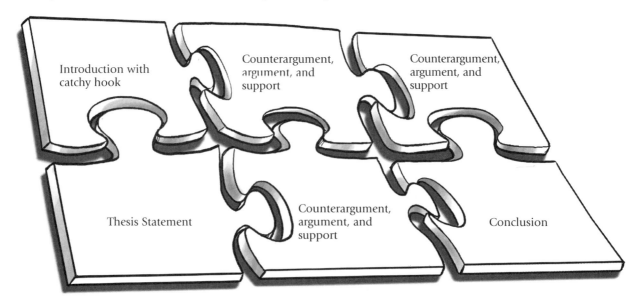

A Add support

THE RIGHT SUPPORT

When you make a claim, you need to support it. Different types of statements may require different types of support. For example, if your essay claims that experts agree on a certain fact, then it would be good to quote a specific expert on that fact. If you claim that a large number of students miss breakfast before school, you could report on your personal experience and that of your friends.

An essay always needs strong support.

Practice 7

Read this draft of a persuasive essay on euthanasia. The student could improve this essay by adding support to various statements throughout the essay. Read the supporting sentences on the next page and identify the best place to put each piece of support.

A Way Out

¹Euthanasia, or mercy killing, should be a choice for a patient who has an incurable disease and doesn't want to live anymore. ²A doctor should be able to help a patient die by injecting or giving a lethal drug. ³This is a very controversial idea, and many people say it is unethical for a doctor to kill someone. ⁴I believe that euthanasia should be legal because it is a way for people to end their own suffering.

⁵Some suffering in life may be a normal thing that a person must learn to accept. ⁶It is also true that some suffering can be addressed with pain-killers

---

continued

or therapy. [7]However, some suffering cannot be relieved by drugs. [8]For patients who are in such pain, every day is just a terrible struggle.

[9]There are several countries around the world that allow organizations or doctors to help patients to die. [10]In parts of the United States, such as the state of Oregon, people are also beginning to recognize the importance of legalizing physician-assisted suicide. [11]As the population of the United States ages, this is going to become a bigger and bigger issue with more and more of the elderly wanting to end their lives painlessly.

Adapted from an essay by Stacy Lee

a Both the Netherlands and Belgium, for example, started to allow physician-assisted suicide in 2002.

After which sentence could you add this *example* support? _____

b On the other hand, I have watched a close relative die in terrible pain, and for me, it was unethical to allow such pain.

After which sentence could you add this *personal experience* support? _____

c One reason is that we know the population is going to keep aging and that by 2050, 25 percent of the U.S. population will be over 85 years old.

After which sentence could you add this *reason* support? _____

d This is called Physician-Assisted Suicide or PAS.

After which sentence could you add this *fact* support? _____

e We must stop the suffering of these patients and stop the suffering of their families and friends who have to watch them.

After which sentence could you add this *emotion* support? _____

Without strong support, your essay is headed for disaster!

B Benefit from peer feedback

Exchange essays and books with a partner. Fill out the form below about your partner's essay. Then return the book and discuss your answers.

PEER FEEDBACK FORM

Writer's name: _____ Date: _____

Reviewer's name: _____

1 On your partner's paper, underline the thesis statement <u>twice</u>.

2 Answer these questions about the thesis statement. Mark each ✓ or X

☐ Is the thesis statement in the introduction?
☐ Does the thesis statement contain a course of action, implied or stated?

3 Underline the topic sentence of each body paragraph <u>once</u>.

4 What types of support are used in each body paragraph?

Body paragraph 1: _____

Body paragraph 2: _____

Body paragraph 3: _____

5 Which are the writer's strongest and weakest arguments?

Strongest: _____

Weakest: _____

6 Can you think of any other persuasive arguments to support the writer's position?

_____

7 Does the writer consider and address counterarguments for each argument? If not, what other counterarguments do you think the writer should consider?

_____

8 Answer these questions about the conclusion. Mark each ✓ or X.

☐ Does the conclusion summarize the main points of the essay?
☐ Does the conclusion end with a strong concluding statement?

9 Draw a star (★) in the margin next to your favorite sentences. Choose two or three. Put a question mark (?) next to any sentences that you didn't understand.

10 Any other comments: _____

_____

_____

C Improve the conclusion

> **CONCLUDING STATEMENTS**
>
> In the same way that an introduction needs to start with a good hook to catch the attention of the reader, a good conclusion should end with a powerful *concluding statement*. The concluding statement is the writer's last chance to persuade the reader. It leaves the reader with a final, provocative thought.
>
> There are many ways to write a memorable close to an essay. A concluding statement can be:
> - a question
> - a call to action
> - an interesting quotation
> - a logical extension of the topic
> - a prediction about the future

Practice 8

Which of the four concluding statements do you think best completes this conclusion to an essay about meditation? Write the letter on the line. Discuss your answer with a partner.

> Everybody should meditate on a regular basis; it is good for one's health and even good for the planet. You can meditate just by sitting quietly for a few moments by yourself. Or you can practice a formal set of routine practices. When meditation is practiced as part of a routine, it's an excellent way to develop oneself. Through meditation, we can focus our minds and grow as human beings. _____

a Most important, meditation can help to focus our minds on greater goals for the common good, such as world peace.

b As the poet Robert Louis Stevenson said, "Quiet minds cannot be perplexed or frightened, but go on in fortune or misfortune at their own private pace, like a clock during a thunderstorm."

c Considering what it offers us, I recommend that everybody try to schedule a specific time for meditation at least three times a week.

d Now that you know what meditation can offer, are you willing to give it a try?

Your turn

Reread your conclusion. Write down two or three possible concluding statements for your essay. Decide which one is most memorable.

D Make revision decisions

Reread your essay and think about your partner's peer feedback. Mark any changes that you want to make on your paper.

E Write the second draft

Use the notes you wrote on your first draft to make revisions. Write the second draft of your essay.

IV EDITING YOUR WRITING

A Edit for modals

MODALS AND MODAL ALTERNATIVES

In a persuasive essay, the writer usually states why it is advisable or necessary for the reader to accept the essay's thesis. Two common ways to express advice and necessity in English are with modal verbs. These verbs can be tricky to use correctly. There are also some effective alternatives to using modals. Using them can offer some variety to your essay.

Modals	Modal alternatives
should	It is important that . . .
ought to	It is essential that . . .
must	It is necessary that . . .

Practice 9

Edit the following paragraph for the correct use of modals. There are five errors.

> Good dental care will keep your teeth healthy and attractive. First, you should eat right. You don't should eat too many foods that are high in sugar. Next, you must care for your teeth well. Ideally, you should to brush your teeth after each meal. However, often this is not practical. At a minimum, you ought brush twice a day: morning and night. In addition to brushing, you should floss your teeth once a day. You must floss in order to clean between the teeth and to

continued

keep your gums healthy. When you floss, you must to be careful to floss deep at the gum line. Finally, you should to have regular check-ups at the dentist's. In these ways, you can keep your teeth healthy and your smile bright for years to come.

Practice 10

The paragraph below is an earlier draft of the fourth paragraph of the essay "Bringing Babies Back to Japan" on pages 91-92. In the draft, underline the modals. Then look at the paragraph on pages 91-92 and note how the writer changed the modals to add variety.

Even though the raising of children is not an easy job or a traditional job for Japanese men, we must accept that it is partly men's work, too. Japanese fathers ought to help more in the home. After all, the children are theirs, too. Also, the Japanese government and companies should set up a better system of parental leave so that both parents can care for their families. My brother-in-law, for example, didn't take his parental leave because he thought it would hurt his career. I have heard many similar stories. Taking parental leave should not threaten a man's job security. In Norway, for instance, men can and do take paternity leave without concern for their careers. Perhaps Japanese companies should consider making paternity leave a requirement so that there can be no question about its impact on one's career. Paternity leave is important because it helps families to understand the father's role sooner, when babies are young.

Practice 11

Rewrite the paragraph in *Practice 9* on page 107 and this page by replacing modals in some of the sentences with modal alternatives. Changing five modals, for example, will give the paragraph greater variety.

Your turn ∿

Read through your second draft. Fix any modals that you may have used incorrectly. If you have overused certain modals, try replacing them with modal alternatives.

B Benefit from peer editing

> **PEER FEEDBACK**
>
> Remember it is often easier to see errors in other students' writing than in your own. It is often a good idea to let a partner read your essay and look for errors that you may have missed. Editing a partner's paper is also a good way to sharpen your own editing skills.

Exchange drafts with a partner. Read your partner's draft and check it for modals and alternatives to modals. Also, look for other grammar or usage issues that seem unusual. Circle anything that you have a question about and put a quesion mark next to it.

C Write the final draft

Write the final draft. As you write, make sure that your spelling, punctuation, and formatting are correct. Check for any grammar errors.

V FOLLOWING UP

A Share your writing

Let's look at the persuasiveness of your writing. After all, the purpose of a persuasive essay is to convince readers. Follow these steps.

1 Write your thesis statement on a separate sheet of paper. Have a partner read your thesis statement (but not your essay) and indicate whether he or she agrees with it, using the following scale.

0	1	2	3	4	5
disagree	mostly disagree	partly agree	agree 50%	mostly agree	completely agree

2 Have your classmate read your entire essay. After reading the essay, your classmate should again indicate agreement on the above scale.

3 Repeat this activity with two or three classmates. Do you feel that your essay has achieved its goal of persuading readers?

B Check your progress

After you get your essay back from your instructor, complete the *Progress Check* below.

PROGRESS CHECK

Date: _____

Essay title: _____

Things I did well in this essay:

_____

_____

_____

Things I want to work on in my next essay:

_____

_____

_____

Look at your *Progress Check* on page 87 of Chapter 3. How did you improve your writing in this essay?

_____

_____

_____

Responding to a Reading

Y ou probably read something every day: an article in a newspaper, a magazine, or a Web site. But how often do you stop and ask yourself, "Is this true? What do I think about what the author is saying?"

In this chapter, you will read an article critically and respond to it in an essay. You will learn how to paraphrase the author's ideas and how to use direct quotes.

A Think about the sample essay topic

You are going to read an essay in response to a magazine article about privacy of information. People worry that if their personal information is not protected, there can be identify theft, which happens when someone uses your name and personal information to steal money or commit other crimes. Before you read the essay, look at the chart below. Then discuss the questions that follow.

Figure 5.1 Sources of identity theft

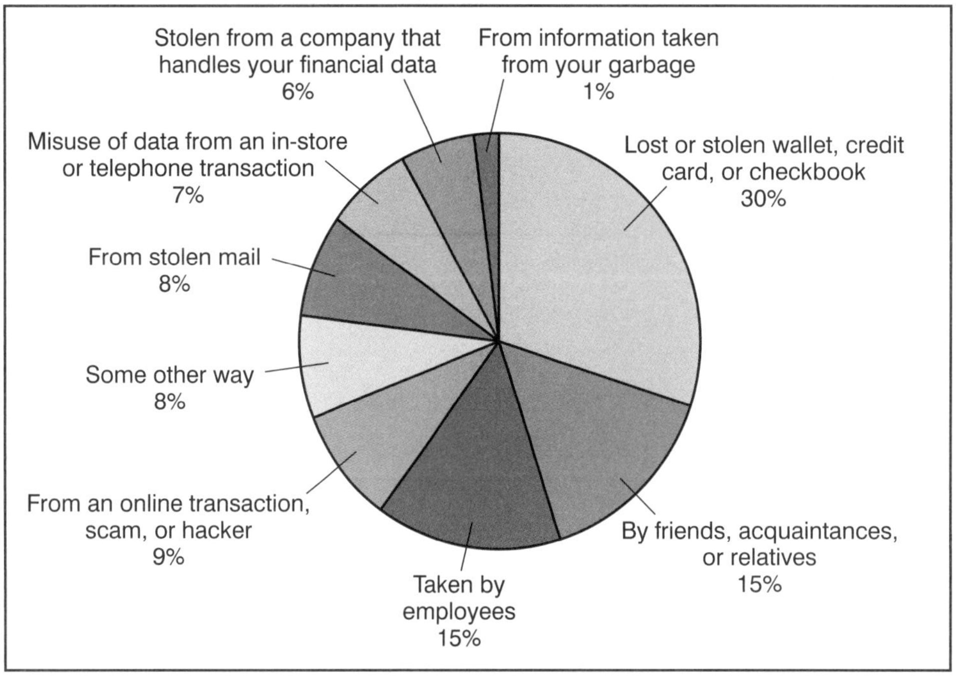

Stolen from a company that handles your financial data
6%

From information taken from your garbage
1%

Misuse of data from an in-store or telephone transaction
7%

Lost or stolen wallet, credit card, or checkbook
30%

From stolen mail
8%

Some other way
8%

From an online transaction, scam, or hacker
9%

By friends, acquaintances, or relatives
15%

Taken by employees
15%

Source: Javelin Strategy & Research 2006

1 According to Figure 5.1, what are the most common ways in which identity is stolen?

2 What data from Figure 5.1 surprise you?

3 Answer these questions. Mark each box (✓) or X.
 ☐ Would you buy a product online with a credit card?
 ☐ Would you have a personal Web page that showed your real name?
 ☐ Would you have your home address and phone number on your Web page?
 ☐ Would you have your photo on your Web page?
 ☐ Would you give out your credit card, ID, or bank account number to someone over the phone?

4 Do you worry about someone stealing your name or personal information? If not, why not? If so, what steps do you take to protect your information?

5 Do you think identity theft is a bigger problem now than it was 15 years ago? Why or why not?

B Read the sample essay

Read the magazine article "The End of Privacy," on pages 159–161. Then read this student essay responding to the article. As you read the essay, decide if the essay is mostly about the opinions in the magazine article or mostly about the writer's own opinions. Then share your ideas with a partner.

Be Careful About Convenience

Life has become very easy. You can buy whatever you want in one second online. Your money is a small card in your pocket that you use to purchase things or get some cash. You can talk to your family or friends almost anytime from almost anywhere using your cell phone. These are useful and convenient additions to our lives. However, you have to give out information about yourself whenever you use these amazing services. The question now is: How safe are you with all this personal information and secrets out there? Are there any laws to protect your privacy? How can you protect these data taken from you by many service providers? In an article published in *Forbes* magazine, Adam Penenberg points out that as e-commerce grows, "marketers and busybodies can access more consumer data than ever before" (159). Easy access to personal information is a serious and growing problem. We need to tighten security so that people can enjoy the benefits that technology brings.

In his article, Penenberg reports that he challenged Dan Cohn of Docusearch.com, a Web detective agency, to get as much information about him as he could. It didn't take Cohn very much time before he could report back to Penenberg with almost all the information and secrets Penenberg would not tell anybody about. This is really scary. No one can feel secure if their personal private data that they used to get some services can easily be given to somebody they don't know and without their permission. What kind of privacy do people still have then? In addition, your personal information can be used against you. You might find yourself bankrupted.

The problem is that U.S. law does not protect this kind of consumer privacy. David Banisar, a Washington, D.C., lawyer who helped set up the Electronic Privacy Information Center, explains that there isn't any universal law to protect consumer privacy in the United States (Penenberg 160-161). However, some other countries have laws to control giving consumers' personal data to others without their permission.

I believe that you must be very careful when you apply for any service that can be used online. Do not give out information that is not needed. Make sure that your service provider will not give your information to strangers. Beware of using online shopping sites that are not trustworthy. Do not give your personal information to anyone online. Penenberg advises, "If you open a bank account with no credit attached to it, ask the bank to keep your Social Security number from credit bureaus. Make sure your broker can – and will – restrict telephone access to your account" (161).

In spite of all these frightening factors, you can still receive many benefits from the convenient services that are provided online. You just need to

continued

be very careful. You should know what information to give, how much information to give, and when and to whom to give it. After that, you can save time and effort and enjoy using such conveniences as credit cards, online shopping, or prepaid telephone cards.

Work Cited

1. Penenberg, Adam L. "The End of Privacy." <u>Forbes</u> (29 November 1999). 25 February 2007 <http://members.forbes.com/forbes/1999/1129/6413182a.html>.

Adapted from an essay by Ali Al Agri

C Notice the essay structure

RESPONSE ESSAYS

College and university students are frequently asked to read an article by an authority on a certain subject and then respond to it in an essay. They are usually either asked to give their opinions on the article or to use the information in the article to support their own opinion on a topic.

This type of essay writing involves a balance between writing your own opinions and summarizing and commenting on someone else's opinions. You can agree or disagree with the article you are responding to, as long as you support your arguments with logical reasons and examples.

In a response essay, you use information from the article you've read, either by quoting its exact words or by paraphrasing the information.

Practice 1

Answer the questions about "Be Careful About Convenience." Then discuss your answers with your classmates.

1 Is the writer evaluating Penenberg's ideas or using Penenberg's evidence to support his own ideas?

2 Underline the thesis statement <u>twice</u>.

3 What type of essay is this (explanatory, problem/solution, comparison-contrast, persuasive, or a combination)?

4 In which paragraph does the writer first mention Penenberg's article?

5 How many examples or pieces of information from "The End of Privacy" does the student writer mention? Underline and number them. How many are direct quotes?

6 What is the student writer's opinion? How is it similar to Penenberg's opinion? How is it different?

7 Look at "The End of Privacy" again. What is your opinion of Penenberg's article? If you were to write a response to Penenberg's article, what additional or different information from his article would you include in an essay about this topic?

D Select an article

Look at the articles in the Appendix (pages 162–165). Skim them (read them quickly) to choose one to which you would like to respond. Which topic interests you the most? Which topic do you have your own ideas about?

You can agree or disagree with the author's main ideas, or even agree with some ideas and not others. Check (✓) the title of the article you intend to use.

_____ "Don't Shoot: Why Video Games Really Are Linked to Violence"

_____ "Kids May Be Right After All: Homework Stinks"

E Brainstorm

USING DISCUSSIONS TO BRAINSTORM

Before you can write a response to an article, you need to both thoroughly understand the article and formulate your own opinions about the information and ideas in the article. Talking with your classmates is an excellent way to explore and clarify your own ideas, learn new ideas from others, and prepare to write.

Follow these guidelines in a group discussion.

- Make sure all group members get the chance to speak and share their ideas.
- Group members do not need to agree. However, everyone should explain his or her ideas clearly, with support and examples where possible.
- Take notes during the discussion. Write down ideas and expressions you may want to use in your essay.

Practice 2

Have a discussion with three to five students who are planning to write about the same article. Discuss the questions below and take notes.

1 Without looking back at the original article, state the article's thesis.
2 What are the author's main ideas that support the thesis? State them in your own words. (You may look back at the article.)
3 What do you think was the author's strongest or most convincing support?
4 What ideas of the author's did you agree with? What ideas did you disagree with? Explain why.
5 Do you know other evidence that supports or does not support the author's points?
6 What is your own opinion on the subject of the article? Why?

Your turn ↝

Now that you have discussed the article, read the two essay assignments below. Choose one for your response essay. Then use one of the brainstorming techniques you have learned (listing, freewriting, creating a Venn diagram, double-listing, discussing) to formulate your own response.

1 Respond to the author's opinions. Choose several of the author's major points. For each one, give a brief summary or explanation of the author's idea, evaluate the author's support, and then say whether you agree or disagree and why.

2 Give your own opinion about the topic. Support your opinion with examples from the article.

▌▌ PREPARING THE FIRST DRAFT

A Compose the thesis statement

STATING YOUR POSITION

Even when you are responding to an article, you should compose a thesis statement that focuses on your own position or opinion. You might agree or disagree with the thesis of the article you read, but your own ideas must be apparent in your thesis statement.

Note that it is not always necessary to mention the article that you are responding to in your thesis statement. In fact, it is possible that you may choose not to mention the article in the introduction at all.

Practice 3

Read the three paragraphs on the next page. They are incomplete introductory paragraphs from student essays responding to "The End of Privacy" on pages 159–161. The paragraphs are missing their thesis statements. Complete each paragraph with the correct thesis statement below. Compare your answer with a partner and then discuss how the rest of the essay might continue. Will the writer mainly agree or mainly disagree with Penenberg's position?

a This is terrible for all individuals, because it means that every one of us is in danger.

b Sometimes, therefore, it is necessary for the government to have access to people's private information, especially for two main reasons: to stop terrorism and to combat financial crimes.

c Unfortunately, however, with the development of computers and the Internet, it has become easier for some dishonest people to access this information as well.

1 _____

Privacy can be defined as having one's information protected from or not available to other people's access. This could be personal or business information that you may want to keep secret from the public. Of course, we expect that some businesses, such as our banks, utility companies, and credit card companies, will have access to some of our personal information.

2 _____

In his article "The End of Privacy," Adam Penenberg points out that it was easy for someone to obtain his private information. It took a Web detective just five minutes to find Penenberg's private data; for example, his birthdate, address, and Social Security number.

3 _____

Life in society would not be possible if there were no laws protecting people or if the government didn't set rules of behavior that tell people what they can or cannot do. This organization of societies allows everyone to live safely. When people don't respect the law or commit crimes, the government needs to be able to investigate.

Your turn

Write your thesis statement. Make sure it clearly shows your opinion.

B Make an outline

Make an outline for your essay similar to the one on the right. Then complete it by writing key words, phrases, and ideas. Remember that you can fill in an idea for your hook later. Add support for each point.

| **I. INTRODUCTION** |
| Hook |
| Background |
| Thesis statement |
| **II. FIRST MAIN IDEA** |
| Support |
| **III. SECOND MAIN IDEA** |
| Support |
| **IV. THIRD MAIN IDEA** |
| Support |
| **V. CONCLUSION** |

C Write your introduction

Now that you know your main ideas, write your introduction. Remember to include a hook, some background information that briefly explains the issue, and your thesis statement. Include a statement that shows the scope of your essay (a preview of the main ideas).

D Critical thinking

CHOOSING SUPPORT FROM AN ARTICLE

Whether you use the article to support your own idea, or write an essay reacting to the article, you'll want to use examples from the article. It's important to choose examples that are strong, interesting, or that explain an important point. Sometimes you may want to paraphrase from the article; sometimes you may choose to use a direct quote.

When to paraphrase:

- The author's information is important, but the exact words he or she used are not special.
- You only need to quote part of an author's long sentence.

When to use a direct quote:

- The author expresses something especially well.
- The author uses unique words, technical terms, or words in a special way.
- You can't think of a way to paraphrase the author's words without changing the meaning.

Practice 4

Read the following direct quotes from "The End of Privacy." With a partner, decide which are important or interesting enough to be used in an essay. Which would you keep as direct quotes? Which would you paraphrase? Different people may make different choices, but be able to explain the reasons for your answers.

1 The phone rang and a stranger sang at the other end of the line, "Happy birthday to you."
   a use and quote directly
   b use and paraphrase
   c do not use

2 Then Daniel Cohn, Web detective, told me the rest of my "base identifiers" – my birthdate, address in New York, Social Security number.
   a use and quote directly
   b use and paraphrase
   c do not use

3 Computers now hold half a billion bank accounts, half a billion credit card accounts, hundreds of millions of mortgages and retirement funds and medical claims and more.

   a use and quote directly

   b use and paraphrase

   c do not use

4 You may well ask: What's the big deal?

   a use and quote directly

   b use and paraphrase

   c do not use

5 Cohn and a team of researchers work out of the top floor of a dull, five-story office building in Boca Raton, Florida, taking orders from 9 a.m. to 4 p.m.

   a use and quote directly

   b use and paraphrase

   c do not use

6 He says the law lets licensed investigators use such tricks as "pretext calling," or fooling company employees into giving out information about customers over the phone (legal in all but a few states).

   a use and quote directly

   b use and paraphrase

   c do not use

7 How did Cohn get my bank secrets? Directly from the source.

   a use and quote directly

   b use and paraphrase

   c do not use

8 In the meantime, I'm starting over: I will change all of my bank, utility, and credit-card account numbers and apply for new unlisted phone numbers.

   a use and quote directly

   b use and paraphrase

   c do not use

Your turn ↻

Go back to the article you chose (pages 162–165). Underline three to five pieces of information that will support your thesis. You may decide later whether to quote or paraphrase that information in your essay.

E Paraphrase an author's opinions

PARAPHRASING

Paraphrase information when the author's information is important, but the exact words are not. When you paraphrase, you need to put the information in your own words. You also need to show the reader where the information came from (or who said or wrote it).

Putting the information in your own words is not always easy! First, you must be sure that you really understand the information completely. Can you look away from the original article and explain the information to someone else? If so, you're ready to paraphrase. Make the following changes when you paraphrase.

- Change the grammar of the original sentence.
- Use different examples.
- Replace individual words with synonyms.

Changing the grammar is the best way to paraphrase. Just replacing a few words with synonyms is not enough, though it can be used with other methods. A paraphrase can be shorter or longer than the original or use more or fewer sentences.

Practice 5

Read each quotation and the three paraphrases. Work with a partner to decide which paraphrases are acceptable and which are not. Discuss what is wrong with the unacceptable paraphrases.

1 "Love many, hate few, learn to paddle your own canoe." – American proverb
- **a** An American proverb tells us to love a lot of people, hate a small number of people, and to know how to drive our own boats.
- **b** The well-known American saying stresses getting along with people as well as being independent.
- **c** Self-reliance and good social skills are typical American values, as can be seen from a popular proverb.

2 "The great thing about a computer notebook is that no matter how much you stuff into it, it doesn't get bigger or heavier." – Bill Gates
- **a** Gates likes laptop computers because you can put a lot of information into them, but they don't increase in size or weight.
- **b** When you store information on paper, such as in notebooks or textbooks, adding more information means adding more pages, and thus more weight. However, as Gates points out, adding more information to a computer does not result in a larger physical product.
- **c** The good thing about a laptop is that however much data you put into it, it doesn't get any larger or weigh more.

3 "Part of the inhumanity of the computer is that, once it is competently programmed and working smoothly, it is completely honest." – Isaac Asimov

    a Computers do not lie or shade the truth, as people do.

    b According to Asimov, computers seem inhuman because, after they are up and running, they always tell the truth.

    c As Asimov reminds us, computers are never capable of telling lies, which is one reason that they will never be fully human!

F Cite an article

> ### CITING AN ARTICLE
>
> When you use someone else's idea, you need to show whose idea it is and where you found it. This is called *citation*. There are different ways to cite works in academic writing, and you should follow the style that your instructor requires. In this chapter, you will follow the Modern Language Association (MLA) style for citing an article.
>
> Here are two common ways to cite paraphrased information. Notice that the author's name is put in parentheses if it is not mentioned in the sentence. The page number is indicated inside parentheses at the end of the sentence.
>
> Penenberg claims that Social Security numbers were not intended to be used for identification at first (161).
>
> When they were first introduced, Social Security numbers were not used to identify people (Penenberg 161).

Practice 6

Work with a partner. Paraphrase and cite the following statements from the three articles in the Appendix on pages 159–165. Then compare your work with another pair of students.

1 "For decades, information like this was kept in large mainframe computers that were difficult to access." (Penenberg, page 159)

_____

_____

2 "Advances in search techniques and the rise of massive databases leave you vulnerable." (Penenberg, page 159)

_____

_____

3 "Congress might pass a bill to outlaw pretext calling. But more than 100 privacy bills filed in the past two years have gone nowhere." (Penenberg, page 161)

_____

_____

4   "Maybe aggressive people are simply more apt to play violent games in the first place." (Schaffer, page 162)

_____

_____

5   "In playing the games, kids are likely to become desensitized to violent, bloody images, which could make them less disturbing and perhaps easier to deal with in real life." (Schaffer, page 163)

_____

_____

6   "Equally important, however, is what the research *doesn't* show: namely, that homework is necessary or beneficial." (Kohn, page 164)

_____

_____

7   "In short, the research provides no reason to think that students would be at any sort of disadvantage if they got much less homework – or maybe even none at all." (Kohn, page 165)

_____

_____

G Quote an author

QUOTING

Quote an article directly when you feel that it has used special language that you would like to present without any changes. It is also good to quote information that is surprising or unusual so that you can show where that information came from.

Here are some common ways to introduce a direct quote. Notice that you use the person's full name the first time you refer to him or her. After that, you use just the last name.

According to Adam Penenberg, "Originally, Social Security numbers weren't used for identification purposes" (161).

"Originally, Social Security numbers weren't used for identification purposes," Penenberg explains (161).

Practice 7

Read the following quotes from "The End of Privacy." Imagine you want to use them in an essay. You may quote some or all of the information. Include a citation. Then share your sentences with a partner or small group.

1 "It's far worse than you think." (page 159)

_____

_____

2 "We have willingly given up some privacy in exchange for convenience; it is why we used a credit card to shop, even though it means we receive more junk mail." (page 159)

_____

_____

3 "Their Web site is open 24 hours a day, 365 days a year. You click through it and load up an online shopping cart as casually as if you were at Amazon.com." (page 160)

_____

_____

4 "For the most part, Cohn's methods are not illegal." (page 160)

_____

_____

5 "With this information, Cohn next got access to a Federal Reserve database that told him where I had bank deposits. Then he located my bank account: my account balance, direct deposits from work, withdrawals, ATM visits, check numbers with dates and amounts, and the name of my broker." (page 160)

_____

_____

Your turn

Look at your article and the ideas that you underlined. Write a _Q_ by the ones you plan to quote. Write a _P_ by the ones you plan to paraphrase.

H Write the first draft

In this section, you have written your thesis statement and introduction. Now write the body paragraphs with at least four examples of paraphrased or cited information from the article you chose. Write a conclusion and add a title. Put these pieces together to create the first draft of your essay.

A Benefit from peer feedback

Exchange essays and books with a partner. Fill out the form below about your partner's essay. Then return the book and discuss your answers.

PEER FEEDBACK FORM

Writer's name: _____ Date: _____

Reviewer's name: _____

1 Underline the thesis statement <u>twice</u>.

2 Answer these questions about the introduction. Mark each box ✓ or X.
   ☐ Does the introduction have an interesting hook?
   ☐ Does the introduction include background information?
   ☐ Does the thesis statement tell you the topic and the writer's opinion?
   ☐ Is there a sentence that shows the scope of the essay?

3 Underline the topic sentence of each body paragraph.

4 How many quotes did the writer use? _____

   How many times did the writer paraphrase information? _____

   Are citations included in parentheses? _____

5 How was the balance between the information from the article and the writer's own opinions? Mark each box ✓ or X.
   ☐ too little information from the article
   ☐ just enough information from the article
   ☐ too much information from the article
   ☐ too few of the writer's own opinions
   ☐ just enough of the writer's own opinions
   ☐ too many of the writer's own opinions

6 What do you think was the writer's strongest argument? What was the writer's best support for that argument?

   _____

   _____

7 Draw a star (★) in the margin by your favorite sentences. Write a question mark (?) in the margin next to any sentences you didn't understand.

8 Any other comments: _____

   _____

   _____

B Check for generalizations

REVISING GENERALIZATIONS WITH HEDGING

A generalization is a statement that declares that something is true for all members of a given group, or in all situations. Generalizations can be dangerous because people and situations are usually quite individual.

As you learned in Chapter 2 (page 60), you can soften generalizations by hedging.

- Use adverbs and expressions of frequency, but avoid *always* and *never*.
- Use modals such as *may, might,* and *can*.
- Use quantifiers, but avoid *all* and *none*.
- Use qualifying phrases such as *it is likely that* and *tend to*.

Practice 8

Read the following body paragraph from a student's essay about "The End of Privacy." First, underline any generalizations that you think are too strong. Then soften them. Compare your results with a partner.

> It is dangerous to use the Internet for shopping. Sites always ask for credit card information and all of your other personal information such as your address and telephone number. Computer experts "hack," or illegally break into, companies' Web sites and steal their customers' information. Then customers not only lose all their money but risk identify theft. I know people who have had problems with information stolen in this way. Companies should collect personal information over the phone, not on their Web sites.

Your turn ↶

Check the language in your essay. Are there any generalizations? If they seem too broad, add language to soften them.

C Use a variety of reporting verbs

REPORTING VERBS

To make your writing more interesting, use a variety of reporting verbs to show what a person said or wrote. Use different verbs depending on the impression you are trying to convey.

- You think that the author is correct.

  show
  prove
  demonstrate

- You think that the author is incorrect.

  claim
  assert
  maintain

- You are neutral. You don't indicate how you feel about the author.

  explain
  report
  describe

Many other verbs can be used as more accurate and interesting synonyms for *say*, such as *add, agree, argue, complain, demand, explain, note, point out, respond, urge.*

Practice 9

Look back at the sample essay "Be Careful About Convenience" on pages 113–114. Find and circle language that shows what a person said or wrote.

Practice 10

Read the paragraph. Change each *say* and *says* to more accurate and interesting verbs. Use verbs from the box *Reporting Verbs* or use other verbs you know.

> High school students these days say they have too much homework. They say they don't have enough time for other activities, such as sports and music, because they are too busy. Many parents say the same. They say their children don't get enough sleep and are even skipping meals. Some teachers, however, say that homework is essential for students. In fact, recent studies say that most teachers assign only two to three hours of homework per week. Some teachers say students are too busy because they do too many outside activities or do not know how to budget their time wisely.

Your turn ∿

Read your essay again. Did you use accurate, interesting, and varied reporting verbs? Circle any examples of *say* or other reporting verbs you are not satisfied with, and write two alternatives above them.

D Write a bibliography

CITING AN ARTICLE

A bibliography is a list of outside sources that you used to write your essay. It is written on a separate sheet of paper, and is the final section of your essay.

In this chapter, you used just one source, so your bibliography will cite one entry. If you use more than one entry in a future essay, remember to list them in alphabetical order by author's last name.

Study this example of a bibliography that cites Penenberg's article:

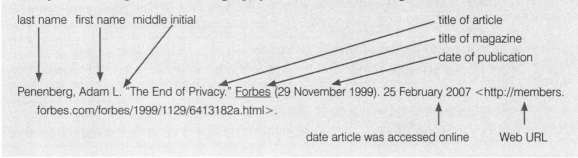

Practice 11

Write bibliography entries here for both "Don't Shoot: Why Video Games Really are Linked to Violence" and "Kids May Be Right After All: Homework Stinks." Use the format shown in the box *Citing an Article*.

1 _____

_____

2 _____

_____

E Make revision decisions

Reread your essay and think about your partner's peer feedback. Mark any other changes that you want to make on your paper.

F Write the second draft

Use the notes you wrote on your first draft to make revisions. Write the second draft of your essay and add a bibliography page.

A   Check for variety of sentences

> ### SENTENCE VARIETY
>
> Good sentence variety, or using diverse structures in sentences, makes your writing more interesting to read.
>
> The basic English sentence contains a subject and a verb and possibly an object, most often in that order.
>
> | | S | V | O |
> |---|---|---|---|
>
> **Basic structure:**   Some credit card companies charge unreasonable fees.
>
> Because this basic sentence is easy to produce, beginning writers sometimes overuse it. Consider what would happen if all sentences followed the $S + V + O$ pattern: The essay would seem boring or unsophisticated.
>
> There are many ways to vary sentences, such as starting with a prepositional phrase, combining clauses, using participial phrases, using transitions, and so on.
>
> - **Prepositional phrase:**   For each overseas transaction, a customer is charged a fee to convert the foreign currency.
> - **Combined clauses:**   Even though I paid my bill in full, I was charged a high interest rate.
> - **Participial phrase:**   Reading my bill carefully, I found service charges that I had not expected.

Practice 12

With a partner, read the paragraphs from two separate student essays. Which paragraph has the most sentence variety? In that paragraph, underline the words and phrases that add variety and interest.

Paragraph A

> Should you pay your credit card bill every month? Surprisingly, your credit card company might not want you to. If you pay your bill late, you will first be charged a late fee. In addition to this, you will be charged interest on the money you owed on your bill. Interest rates can be as high as 20 percent or more, and late fees seem to increase every year. By paying your bill in full every month, you avoid these charges and pay only for your purchases. However, you don't need to feel sorry for the credit card companies. Each time you use your card to purchase an item or a service, the credit card company receives a fee from the business that sold to you.

Paragraph B

> Many people enjoy using credit cards when they travel abroad. Credit cards are convenient. There are some dangers with using credit cards. Credit card companies charge fees to convert currencies. They also charge their own fees for each overseas transaction. These fees are then more expensive than bank fees. Customers also don't expect the transaction fees. They feel surprised when they see their credit card bills after their trip. Travelers checks might help you control your travel budget better.

Practice 13

Complete the paragraph below about credit cards. Use phrases from the box below to give the paragraph more sentence variety.

Although credit cards are convenient	If you don't want
but also	More expensive than
consider using	not only

> Many people enjoy using credit cards when they travel abroad. _____ , there are some dangers with using them. Credit card companies _____ charge fees to convert currencies, _____ charge their own fees for each overseas transaction. _____ bank fees, these transaction fees are also unexpected. _____ to be surprised by your credit card bills after your trip, _____ travelers checks to help you control your travel budget better.

Your turn 🌊

Edit your essay. Check for sentence variety and mark any places where you want to reword your sentences.

B Edit for punctuation

Study these rules about using punctuation marks with quotations.

If you begin with a phrase and the quotation is a complete sentence:
- Use a comma between the phrase and the opening quotation marks.
- Begin the quoted sentence with a capital letter.
- Put the page number after the quotation marks, in parentheses.
- Put a period after the parentheses.

    Penenberg warns us, "It's far worse than you think" (159).

If the quotation is NOT a complete sentence:
- Don't use a comma before the quotation.
- Don't begin the quotation with a capital letter.

    Penenberg warns us that the situation is "far worse than you think" (159).

If you begin the sentence with a quotation, and finish it with your own words:
- End the quoted sentence with a comma, not a period.
- Put the comma inside the quotation marks.
- Put the page number before the period at the end of the sentence.

    "It's far worse than you think," Penenberg warns us (159).

Put question marks and exclamation points inside the quotation marks only if they belong to the original quotation:

    "Dan Dunn?" the bank employee asked (160).

Practice 14

Add punctuation to the following sentences. The quoted words are underlined.

1 <u>Computers now hold half a billion bank accounts</u> reports Penenberg (page 159)

2 Penenberg poses the question <u>Why should we care if our personal information isn't so personal anymore</u> (page 159)

3 Penenberg explains <u>Docusearch's clients include lawyers, insurers, private detectives, and businesses</u> (page 160)

4 <u>Docusearch's clients include lawyers, insurers, private detectives, and businesses</u> explains Penenberg (page 160)

5 Penenberg claims that Cohn got the author's bank account number <u>directly from the source</u> (page 160)

Your turn ↷

Check the quotes that you used in your essay. Did you use the correct punctuation? Make any necessary changes now.

C Write the final draft

As you write your final draft, make the revisions and edits you have noted. Make sure that your spelling, punctuation, and formatting are correct, and check for any grammar errors.

V FOLLOWING UP

A Share your writing

Work with a group of students who wrote about the same article. Follow these steps.

1 Take turns reading your essays aloud.
2 As you listen, write down a sentence or idea that you especially like.
3 When the reader is finished, tell him or her the sentences that you liked.
4 When everyone has finished reading, discuss how the essays were similar and how they were different. Who agreed with the author? Who disagreed? Did any students choose the same quotations?

B Check your progress

After you get your essay back from your instructor, complete the *Progress Check* below.

PROGRESS CHECK

Date: _____

Essay title: _____

Things I did well in this essay:

_____

_____

_____

Things I need to work on in my next essay:

_____

_____

_____

Look back at your *Progress Checks* from previous chapters. How did you improve your writing in this essay?

_____

_____

_____

Timed Essays

Throughout your life, there will be occasions when you have to write under time pressure. Often these pieces of writing are very important. They can determine if you pass a test, get into college, or even get a job.

In this chapter, you will learn how to be successful in writing timed essays. This process differs from most other writing because you will usually only have time to produce one draft. So, you must learn to outline quickly, write efficiently, and edit neatly.

A Think about timed essays

You are going to read and evaluate a sample timed essay. Before starting, look at the information below about the different types of standardized exams of English that include a timed essay in the writing section. Discuss the questions that follow.

Figure 6.1 Tests of English that include timed essays

Standardized test	Writing section	Time and length
TOEFL (Test of English as a Foreign Language)	Two writing tasks • An opinion essay • A summary of a reading and a lecture	• 20 minutes • 30 minutes • About 250 words each task
IELTS (International English Language Testing System)	Two writing tasks • A written description of some graphic data • An essay supporting a point of view	• 60 minutes total • Task 1 - at least 150 words • Task 2 - at least 250 words
SAT (Scholastic Aptitude Test)	One writing task • An essay supporting a point of view	• 25 minutes
GED (General Educational Development)	One writing task • An opinion essay	• 45 minutes
GRE (Graduate Record Examinations)	Two writing tasks • An essay supporting a point of view • An analysis of an argument	• 45 minutes • 30 minutes
Other tests with timed essays: high school exit exams; college English placement exams; exams for different subject areas	Essays and short answers	Time and length vary.

1 Have you ever taken any of the exams that are listed in the chart? Describe the writing section of the test. What was your experience with the timed writing activity?

2 Have you ever written an in-class essay for an exam? Describe the situation.

3 For you, what is the most difficult part of writing a timed essay? What is the easiest part?

4 What future situations might require you to write a timed essay?

B Read the sample timed essay

As you read the sample timed essay, ask yourself if it directly answers the essay question. In other words, did the writer understand and respond to the question? Then share your answer with a partner.

Directions: Write an essay to answer the question below. Support your opinion with specific examples. You have 30 minutes.

Essay question:
Do you agree or disagree with the following statement?
Grades motivate students to learn.

Grades Motivate Students

by Miwa Sakai

I agree with the idea that grades motivate students to learn. Grades encourage students for several reasons. They help students see their learning progress, reward students, and show a student's position compared to classmates.

First, grades help students see their progress in learning, ~~Because~~ because grades reflect students' efforts in a class. In a grade, students can clearly see the results of their work. In addition, grades are firmer than some vague comments from instructors. When students get an alphabetical grade or number score, they may be encouraged to study harder to get a higher grade.

In addition to inspiring them to work harder, grades may also help students to find interest in a subject. If students earn a desired grade in a class, they may feel happy. and realize that they have talent for the subject. Then they might start to do extra research or reading outside of the class. These ~~works~~ activities may help them to learn even more. So for some students, a grade may be like a reward that encourages more learning.

Most importantly, students like to know that their work is recognized. If a school did not use any grade system, students might feel that even though they studied harder than other students, their effort was not noticed. ~~It's just like being underpaid in a hard job at a fast food restaurant.~~ They might feel that nobody valued their efforts. ~~So~~ so they might not feel like studying.

Grades offer students a solid way to think about their work and their skills. This can motivate students to study more, to find their ~~strenghts~~ strengths, and to feel that their effort is valued. For these reasons, I agree that grades can help students learn.

C Notice features of a timed essay

> **TIMED ESSAYS**
>
> When writing a timed essay, it's important to keep in mind how your essay will be graded or scored. Most timed essays are evaluated in four areas: content, organization, language, and mechanics (spelling and punctuation).
>
> **Content**
> - An introduction with a thesis statement that directly answers the test question
> - Clear and relevant ideas that support the thesis statement
> - A conclusion, however short
>
> **Organization**
> - Logical organization of supporting ideas
>
> **Language**
> - Variety and complexity of sentences
> - Clear transitions between ideas and sentences
> - Appropriate vocabulary
>
> **Mechanics**
> - Proper essay formatting
> - Correct grammar, spelling, and punctuation

Practice 1

Answer these questions about "Grades Motivate Students." Then discuss your answers with a partner.

1 Underline the thesis statement <u>twice</u>. Does it directly answer the exam question?

2 What functions does the introduction serve? Check (✓) as many as apply.

_____ It grabs the reader's attention with an interesting hook.

_____ It gives background information about the topic.

_____ It states the writer's thesis.

_____ It shows the scope of the essay by introducing the main ideas.

3 Look at the content of the body paragraphs. Underline the topic sentence in each paragraph <u>once</u>. Is each topic mentioned in the introduction? Is each topic well-supported in its paragraph?

4 Circle any transition words that are used to link body paragraphs. Is the organization of the essay logical? Why or why not?

5 Look at the concluding paragraph. Do you think it is acceptable for a timed essay? Why or why not?

6 Consider the language in the essay. Is there a good variety of sentence types? Is the vocabulary appropriate?

7 Has the writer paid careful attention to the mechanics of formatting, grammar, spelling, and punctuation?

8 Has the writer produced a double-spaced essay? That is, did he or she write on every other line? Why do you think that is a good idea?

D Follow the writing process

THE WRITING PROCESS FOR A TIMED ESSAY

When you write a timed essay, you will follow the same steps as writing an untimed essay: gathering ideas, organizing your ideas in an outline, writing the essay, and revising it. However, there are several key differences due to the time limit.

- Your outline must be brief, not detailed.
- You will probably only write one draft.
- Any revisions must be minor and must be neatly marked.
- You will need to keep to a strict time schedule as you write. Otherwise, you may not have time to complete your writing or other sections of the test.

Some students think that they can "save time" by skipping a step such as the outline. On the contrary, skipping the outline may cost them time. It can lead to a poorly organized essay with problems that cannot be fixed in the time given.

Practice 2

Think about the process of writing a timed essay compared to an untimed essay. Read the steps below. If the step applies only to a timed essay, circle *a*. Circle *b* for steps only used for untimed essays, or circle *c* for steps used in both timed and untimed essays.

1 Do research and discuss ideas with peers.
  a timed
  b untimed
  c both timed and untimed

2 Think about your thesis.
  a timed
  b untimed
  c both timed and untimed

3 Think about the best possible way to organize your main points.

  a timed

  b untimed

  c both timed and untimed

4 Write a detailed outline.

  a timed

  b untimed

  c both timed and untimed

5 Write and revise the introduction several times until it is nearly perfect.

  a timed

  b untimed

  c both timed and untimed

6 Write a conclusion.

  a timed

  b untimed

  c both timed and untimed

7 Write only one draft of your essay.

  a timed

  b untimed

  c both timed and untimed

8 Reread your essay and make corrections to spelling and grammar.

  a timed

  b untimed

  c both timed and untimed

Practice 3

Imagine that you have 30 minutes to write an essay for an exam. Decide how many minutes you would spend on each of the following. Write the number of minutes in the blank. Discuss your answers with a partner.

_____ **1** Brainstorming ideas and drafting an outline

_____ **2** Writing the introduction

_____ **3** Writing the body paragraphs

_____ **4** Writing the conclusion

_____ **5** Revising and editing

Practice 4

Read each of the following timed essay instructions. Choose the best way to use your time. Then discuss your decisions with a partner.

1 | **Directions:** Write two essays. Choose two of the following five topics.
  | **Total time:** 60 minutes
  | **Points:** Essay 1 = 20 points; Essay 2 = 20 points

  a Write as much as possible in the first essay topic. Use the remaining time for the second topic.

  b Spend 30 minutes on each essay.

  c Spend 20 minutes on Essay 1, 40 minutes on Essay 2.

2 | **Directions:** Write two essays.
  | **Total time:** 90 minutes
  | **Points:** Essay 1 = 75 points; Essay 2 = 25 points

  a Spend 65 minutes on Essay 1, 25 minutes on Essay 2.

  b Spend 50 minutes on Essay 1, 40 minutes on Essay 2.

  c Spend 45 minutes on each essay.

3 | **Directions:** Complete each of the three parts of the test.
  | **Total time:** 120 minutes
  | **Points:**
  | **Part I:** 25 True/False Questions (1 point each)
  | **Part II:** 25 Multiple Choice Questions (1 point each)
  | **Part III:** Essay (50 points)

  a Finish Parts I and II first. Then spend the rest of your time on Part III – the essay.

  b Save at least 60 minutes for the essay.

  c Be careful with your time on Parts I and II. Save at least 40 minutes for the essay.

E Select a question

Choose an exam question from the three listed below. Throughout Sections II, III, and IV of this chapter, you will follow the steps of the writing process to write a 30-minute timed essay on the question you choose. (Because the timed essay-writing steps are practiced and spaced out throughout this chapter, the total writing time for the essay will in fact be slightly longer than 30 minutes.)

1 If you could change one important thing in your city or town, what would you change? Use reasons and specific examples.

2 Do you agree or disagree with the following statement?
Consumers should have to pay for every song they download from the Internet.

3 Discuss the similarities and differences in the student-teacher relationship for young children (grade school) and for young adults (high school through college).

A Understand the test question

> ### UNDERSTANDING THE TEST QUESTION
>
> In every exam, it is always imperative that you read the question carefully and make sure that you understand it before you attempt to answer it. This is particularly true of timed essay exams. Here are four strategies to use when you first receive the essay question.
>
> - Read the question several times.
> - Underline key words in the question that tell you what to write about and how to write about it.
>   > Describe what is meant by Realism, and name two writers whose work marked its beginning. Then discuss the specific features of one of the writers. Explain why the writer is representative of Realism.
> - If the question has several parts, number them.
>   > 1 Describe what is meant by Realism, and 2 name two writers whose work marked its beginning. Then 3 discuss the specific features of one of the writers. 4 Explain why the writer is representative of Realism.
> - Write the question in your own words. This will force you to make sure that you actually understand the question.
>   > Define Realism. Name two early Realist writers. For one of those writers, explain the features in his or her writing that make the writer typical of Realism.

Practice 5

Match some common instruction terms with their meanings.

Instruction terms	Meaning
____ 1 compare and contrast	a talk about different ideas
____ 2 explain	b get the reader to agree with you
____ 3 discuss	c talk about similarities and differences
____ 4 persuade	d select from two or more
____ 5 choose one	e judge how good or bad
____ 6 evaluate	f give reasons; tell what something is like

Practice 6

Underline the key words in the exam question. Then choose the sentence that rephrases the exam question accurately.

1 Explain three ways in which human activities are changing the environment.
   a Describe how people's behavior affects the earth.
   b Propose three ways to slow or reverse the changes in the environment that are being caused by humans.

2 Consider two ways to lose weight: reducing calories or increasing exercise. Which is a more effective way to lose weight, and why?
   a Evaluate which is a better way to lose weight: eating less or exercising more.
   b Talk about a personal experience with weight loss or weight gain.

3 Discuss two major challenges for students today that students probably did not face 50 years ago.
   a Show how technology has changed the classroom in two ways.
   b Compare students' concerns in the twenty-first century to those in the last half of the twentieth century.

4 Read the following article about new ways to break the habit of cigarette smoking. Based on this reading, persuade smokers that they should try quitting because it has gotten easier.
   a Evaluate new innovations that help smokers to quit and determine which would be the most effective.
   b Convince smokers that quitting is now easier to do than it used to be.

Your turn ↜

Look back at the exam question you selected on page 139. Underline the key words. Then rewrite the question in your own words. Compare your rewrite with someone who chose the same question as you.

B Write a rough outline

OUTLINING QUICKLY

Writing a quick outline before writing your essay is like drawing a map for your writing. It can keep you from getting lost as you write. With practice, you should be able to produce a short but effective outline in just a few minutes. After you write your outline, check it by asking yourself the following questions.

- Does the thesis statement directly address the question?
- Does each main idea support the thesis? Are any ideas irrelevant?
- Are the main ideas ordered logically according to the thesis and the topic?
- Can you think of specific ways to support each main idea?

Practice 7

Read the following essay question and two sample outlines. As you read the outlines, consider the following questions. Then discuss your answers with a partner.

1 Does the thesis statement directly answer the question?

2 Do the main points support the thesis statement? Are the main points in a logical order?

3 Which outline is better for a timed essay? Why?

4 Can you think of ways to improve the better outline?

Essay question
Describe how college students in the United States typically prepare for a career path.

Outline A

I. THESIS: IN PREPARING FOR A CAREER, U.S. COLLEGE STUDENTS 1) IDENTIFY THEIR INTEREST, 2) DECLARE THEIR MAJOR IN RELATED FIELD, AND 3) DO ENTRY-LEVEL WORK OR INTERNSHIPS TO GET EXPERIENCE

II. IDENTIFY INTEREST

III. SELECT THEIR MAJOR

IV. GET WORK EXPERIENCE IN FIELD

V. CONC.

Outline B

I. THESIS: WHEN U.S. COLLEGE STUDENTS CHOOSE THEIR CAREER PATH, THEY USUALLY THINK ABOUT WHAT THEY WANT TO DO, TRY TO LEARN ABOUT THEIR OPTIONS BY READING OR TALKING TO PEOPLE, CHOOSE AN APPROPRIATE MAJOR IN COLLEGE, AND FINALLY FIND THEIR FIRST JOB.

II. THINK ABOUT WHAT THEY WANT
  A. INTERESTS
  B. SALARY

III. RESEARCH THEIR OPTIONS
  A. ONLINE AND LIBRARY RESEARCH
  B. TALK WITH PROFESSORS AND PROFESSIONALS

IV. GET WORK EXPERIENCE IN FIELD
  A. INTERNSHIPS
  B. SUMMER JOBS

V. CHOOSE RELATED MAJOR IN COLLEGE
  A. DECIDE BY END OF SECOND YEAR
  B. MEET WITH ADVISOR

VI. CONCLUSION

Practice 8

For each of the following timed essay questions, time yourself while you write an outline in five minutes or less. Include a thesis statement and two or three main ideas. Then compare your outlines in a small group.

1 Explain the differences and similarities between two things that you know well: two sports, two books, two countries' foods, two countries' music, and so on.

2 Do you agree or disagree with the following statement?
Television destroys communication among friends and family.

3 If you could study a subject that you have never studied before, what would you choose? Give details to explain your choice.

Your turn

Follow these steps to start the exam writing process.

1 On a piece of paper, write your exam question from *Select a Question* on page 139.

2 Quickly brainstorm a list of ideas. Then circle several main ideas.

3 Write a brief outline for your essay. Spend only 5 minutes.

4 After 5 minutes, check your outline by asking yourself the questions in the box *Outlining Quickly* on page 141.

C Write an introduction

TIMED ESSAY INTRODUCTIONS

When writing the introduction in a timed essay, keep these points in mind.

- **Length:** The introduction in a timed essay should be short. Three or four sentences should be enough. The purpose of an introduction in a timed essay is to prepare readers for the contents of the essay and to state your thesis.

- **Hook:** A good hook may make a good impression on an examiner reading your essay. However, if a good hook does not come to mind right away, omit one. In timed essays, a hook is less common and not essential.

- **Background:** In a timed essay, if the topic relates to material covered in a class, you can assume that your reader has the required background to follow your essay. Background information is usually not needed. However, if the topic relates to personal experience or your opinion, you may need to provide some background.

Practice 9

Read the following introductions. Evaluate each introduction according to the questions below. Then give each introduction a score between 1 (lowest) and 5 (highest). Discuss your answers with your classmates and explain reasons for each score.

- Is it short?
- Is there a hook? (Remember that a hook isn't necessary, but can add interest.)
- Is there background information? Is it necessary?
- Does the paragraph clearly state the thesis?
- Does the paragraph prepare the reader for the body of the essay?

1 Score: _____

I have been living in the United States a little more than one year, and I have learned about American customs and compared them with those of my country. One of the points that has caught my attention is education. In the United States, I have found many resources and opportunities to study. In Peru, it is not the same. Once I read a newspaper article that said Peru has the most ineffective and inefficient education system in Latin America.

2 Score: _____

I prefer writing a final paper to taking a final exam in my college classes. Writing a final paper is less stressful than taking a test. It gives students a chance to learn new material, rather than just proving what they already know. Most importantly, I tend to score higher on untimed writing than on written exams.

3 Score: _____

One of the biggest minority groups in Vietnam is Cambodian people. Have you ever been to Cambodia? I haven't. Cambodians started coming to Vietnam during their war. It was a crisis for Vietnam because my country wasn't ready for so many immigrants. In my senior year class in high school, there were about 20 Cambodians in a class of 260 students. The crisis in Cambodia was hurting everybody. I think each country should do what it can to help political exiles.

4 Score: _____

Do you worry about the content on the Internet? Internet content is likely to offend many people, especially parents with teenage children. Still, parents shouldn't try to control their teenagers' access to the Internet, because their children are old enough to make their own decisions, and in the end, they will access whatever information they want regardless of their parents' rules.

Your turn ↄ

You spent about five minutes writing an outline for your timed essay. Now spend no more than five minutes writing your introduction. Use your outline to help you. Be sure your introduction prepares the reader for the content of your essay and clearly states your thesis.

D Write the body

CHOOSING SUPPORT

Before writing the body of your essay, you need to plan what kind of support to include for each main idea. Your rough outline may only have a thesis statement and your main ideas. On your outline, note the type of support you will use for each main point before you write the body paragraphs.

The type of support you use will depend on the essay topic. Here are some types of support. (See Chapter 4, page 101.)

- Personal experience
- Expert opinion
- Examples
- Analogy
- Facts and statistics
- Reason
- Emotion

Practice 10

Read the following exam question, the student's thesis statement, and two body paragraphs from the student's essay. Decide what type of support could be added, and complete each paragraph with supporting sentences.

Exam question: *A local high school will receive a large amount of money to spend as it wishes. It will be enough money to build a new building, hire four new teachers, or fund several special programs. Write a persuasive essay about how you think the money should be spent.*

Thesis statement: *The high school should spend the money on an after-school sports program and art classes.*

Although many people believe that Westmont High School should spend this large donation on a new football stadium, an after-school recreational sports program would benefit many more students. There are sports teams for a few top athletes, but there are very few opportunities for students to play sports just for fun. _____

_____

_____

_____

_____ Having a recreational sports program after school would give many students a fun and healthy way to spend the afternoon.

continued

The other type of program that would be an important addition for the high school is an art program. Over the past 10 years, all art classes have been eliminated. This includes drawing, painting, computer graphic design, film, and photography. There are many artistic students, but they have no place to learn and develop artistically. _____

_____

_____

_____

_____

_____ Art classes would give students an opportunity that is missing at Westmont High School.

Your turn ↻

You spent about ten minutes writing an outline and an introduction for your timed essay. Now spend no more than 15 minutes adding your body paragraphs. Use your outline to help you and note what type of support you will use for each of the main points. As you write your body paragraphs, keep the following points in mind.

- Double-space your writing so that you can easily revise it later.
- Start each body paragraph with a clear topic sentence.
- Make sure each main idea has strong support.
- Each sentence should be relevant to the topic. Don't just write to fill space on the page.
- Keep an eye on your time.

E Write a conclusion

TIMED ESSAY CONCLUSIONS

Like the introduction, the conclusion of a timed essay can be short. You should not spend a lot of time writing it. An ideal conclusion for a timed essay might be just three or four sentences. Think of the conclusion as having three parts.

- Restatement of the thesis statement
- Summary of the main points of the essay
- A concluding statement (a suggestion, a prediction, or a closing thought)

Practice 11

Read the following conclusions. Evaluate each one according to the questions below. Then give each conclusion a score between 1 (lowest) and 5 (highest). Discuss your answers with your classmates and explain reasons for each score.

- Is there a sentence that appears to restate the thesis?
- Is it clear from the conclusion what the main points brought up in the essay were?
- Is there unnecessary information?
- Does it end with a concluding statement?
- Is it too short?
- Is it easy to understand?

1 Score: _____

While single-sex high schools have disadvantages, their overall benefits outweigh the drawbacks. They give students confidence and focus, two important traits that students may then use as they enter the professional world.

2 Score: _____

Single-sex high schools may have advantages, such as reducing distraction in class, minimizing the importance of clothing and looks in school, and allowing students to develop their characters and strengths. However, their negative points are even greater than their advantages. For example, students in single-sex schools may not develop socially, they may not know how to compete with members of the opposite sex, and they may not be accustomed to normal environments where men and women work together. I went to a single-sex high school, and overall, it was a negative experience for these reasons.

3 Score: _____

In conclusion, students who use computers to create fancy fonts, formatting, and tables in their schoolwork may be under the misconception that the appearance of their work is more important than its content. This is a dangerous illusion because in most real-world situations, content carries more weight than fancy fonts.

4 Score: _____

Fancy fonts and formatting may look beautiful, but the students who use them are actually hiding behind an embarrassing fact: They have nothing to say. What is the benefit of typing up a pretty document if it doesn't really say anything? Students should spend more time learning information in the first place.

Your turn ↷

You have written an outline, the introduction, and the body paragraphs of your 30-minute timed essay. You have just a couple of minutes left to add a brief conclusion. However, you must still leave about five minutes to read your essay and do some quick revision and editing (see Sections III and IV). Now write your conclusion.

A Revise ideas

> ### MAKING CONTENT CHANGES
>
> Revising the content of a timed essay is difficult because you usually only have time to write one draft. Most timed essays are written by hand, so adding and deleting material can make your paper look messy or hard to read. For these reasons, don't make too many changes to the content.
>
> - Add only content that is necessary or that makes a major contribution to the essay. Do not add information simply because you need to fill the page.
> - Delete material by simply crossing it out with a single, straight line. Remember that many deletions can look messy, so only delete what is truly irrelevant or incorrect.

Practice 12

Read the paragraph from an essay on video games and violence. Follow the steps below to revise ideas.

1 Find one sentence in the paragraph that does not support the topic sentence. Delete it neatly.
2 Add the following sentence to improve this paragraph. Write it as neatly as you can. *Young people who play these games may lose touch with the results of real violence.*

> Playing violent video games has a dangerous effect on young players. These games may encourage the negative emotions of children who already feel angry or isolated. Although most young players are boys, many girls also play video games on a regular basis. In video games, it is acceptable to be violent and angry. It is OK to use a gun and shoot many people. Even being shot is perfectly fine because players are brought back to life with the click of a button. Young players may think that violence is an acceptable solution in the real world.

B Connect ideas

> ## TRANSITIONS
>
> During the pressure of a timed essay, it is easy to forget to use transition words and expressions. However, these words are important because they tie ideas together and connect one sentence to the next, or one paragraph to the next. Transitions guide your reader logically through your essay. These words are often quite easy to add to an essay and can greatly improve its quality.
>
> Add FANBOYS:
>   for, and, not, but, or, yet, so
> Add other transitions:
>   because, for example, for instance, however, therefore

Practice 13

Connect ideas in the sentences below by adding transitions. Neatly make any necessary changes to the sentences and show where to add the transitions. The first one is done for you.

and	because	for example	however	or	so

1 Usually volcano eruptions follow several earthquakes. *However, last* ~~Last~~ month, one eruption occurred after a period with minimal earthquake activity.

2 Usually volcano eruptions follow several earthquakes. In the 24-hour period before the eruption in May, nine earthquakes were recorded.

3 At many U.S. universities, female students dramatically outnumber males. College administrations are considering how to attract more male students.

4 Many students have to decide whether to go to college full-time and take out a student loan. They could go to college part-time and get a job.

5 Dancers develop a sense of balance. They develop a sense of grace.

6 Two of the boys speak Finnish. They study at a Finnish school on the weekends.

Your turn 〰

Revise your essay. Check for irrelevant information, add any important new ideas, and check for transitions between ideas. Mark your revisions neatly.

A Check for run-on sentences

> ### FIXING RUN-ONS
>
> When you write a timed essay, it is not uncommon to write run-on sentences. These sentences consist of two or more independent clauses that are not joined correctly. That is, they may be missing punctuation or transition words.
>
> There are several ways to correct a run-on sentence.
>
> - **Add punctuation**
>   Run-on: Since there is a fee for each college application only apply to colleges that truly interest you.
>   Revision: Since there is a fee for each college application, only apply to colleges that truly interest you.
>
> - **Add transition words**
>   Run-on: Most college applications are due in the fall some colleges have open admissions year-round.
>   Revision: Most college applications are due in the fall. However, some colleges have open admissions year-round.
>   Revision: Most college applications are due in the fall, but some colleges have open admissions year-round.
>
> - **Divide the run-on sentence into two or more shorter sentences**
>   Run-on: Applying to college requires a great deal of planning and organization because you have to read about and choose colleges, then you have to ask teachers for recommendations and write your essay and get your transcripts sent from your school.
>   Revision: Applying to college requires a great deal of planning and organization. First, you have to read about and choose colleges. Then you have to ask teachers for recommendations, write your essay, and get your transcripts sent from your school.

Practice 14

Read the run-on sentences. Fix them according to the suggestion in parentheses. The first one is done for you.

1 Any time I work on my computer for more than three hours, my eyes get tired, my neck hurts, and my shoulders get tight, and usually my mother has to remind me to take a break. (*Divide into two sentences*)

2 Since we live in a large apartment building I know a lot of other kids who are my age and we can always find something to do. (*Add punctuation*)

3 Sometimes I can't answer the teacher's question I know the answer. (*Add transition*)

4 Members of varsity sports teams aren't supposed to hold part-time jobs but it's not legal for the school district to forbid them. (*Add punctuation*)

5 It's not legal for the school district to forbid them to have jobs it's like an unspoken rule. (*Add transition*)

6 Most of the crossword puzzles in this book are so long I can't do them all at once I have to go back once or twice or sometimes even three times to get all the words. (*Add transition and punctuation. Divide into two sentences*)

Practice 15

Read the sentences. If they are fine, write *OK*. If they run on, write *RO* and fix them. Discuss your answers with a classmate.

_____ **1** Mr. Martini's multiple-choice tests were famous for being short but tricky.

_____ **2** The developers typically buy inexpensive land at the edge of a town and wait for the population to grow enough that the inexpensive land becomes a desirable suburb this way they can sell it at a profit.

_____ **3** Trying to do homework in the library while other people are talking or whispering frustrates students and they end up being inconvenienced due to other people's rudeness.

_____ **4** In order to ensure a fair process for selection, each member will write his or her name on a slip of paper and put it into a hat for random drawing.

Your turn

Check your essay for any run-on sentences, and neatly mark changes.

B Edit language

EDITING A TIMED ESSAY

When you write under time pressure, you often make mistakes. Simple errors in language or grammar will decrease your score for an essay exam. Therefore, it is important to leave time at the end to quickly but carefully edit your essay. Check your essay for the following types of errors.

- Spelling
- Punctuation
- Missing words
- Correct verb forms and tense
- Subject-verb agreement
- Academic language instead of informal language

Practice 16

Edit the paragraph below. Check for the errors listed in the box *Editing a Timed Essay*. Insert your changes in neat handwriting.

My homtown, Guiyu, China, recently become the world's biggest electronic garbage dump. The developed world exports its old electronics to Guiyu for reprocessing. In Guiyu, thousands family workshops handle this stuff. While this work provide them cash, residents pay a diferent price for accepting this industry. The price is their health. Bosses don't care about workers' health. They ignore laws, releasing toxic fumes into the air and dumping acid into rivers. Guiyu must recognize the environmental and health hazards of its biggest industry. If the town want to clean up environment and protect the health of its citizen, it will having to strengthen laws for handling waste and punish law breakers.

Your turn

Edit your essay for the errors listed in the box *Editing a Timed Essay* on page 151.

C Add a title

Practice 17

Reread the four introductory paragraphs in Practice 9 on page 144. For each paragraph, imagine the contents of the rest of the essay. Write a short, clear title for each essay. Share your titles with your classmates and explain how you chose your title.

1 *Peru's Inefficient Education System* _____

2 _____

3 _____

4 _____

Your turn

Add a short, clear title to your essay. Don't spend much time on your title – it usually counts little if at all toward the grade of a timed essay.

A Manage stress

MANAGING STRESS

Most students feel some stress about exams. Some stress is expected and can be beneficial. However, too much stress can negatively affect your performance on a test.

If you experience a lot of stress *before* a test, think of ways to relax. Here are some common ways to reduce stress.

- Exercise (for example, walk, swim, play soccer).
- Meditate (for example, close your eyes and imagine a peaceful scene).
- Breathe deeply.
- Play a game.
- Get enough sleep.
- Be well prepared. Know the test format and anticipate what is likely to be on the test.

If you feel stressed *during* an exam, keep the following in mind.

- Understanding and using the writing process will help you manage your time, organize your ideas, and prioritize your writing efforts.
- Keep track of your time, but don't panic. If you are well organized and follow the writing process, you should be able to finish in time.
- Have confidence that you have the tools to write effectively.
- Don't worry about small errors. For a timed essay, nobody expects a perfect paper.

Practice 18

In a small group, discuss these questions about exam stress.

1 Are you more nervous before or during a test?
2 What activities help you manage stress before an exam?
3 What helps you stay relaxed and focused during an exam?
4 Do you have any special tips or advice about reducing exam stress?

B Write a timed essay

REVIEWING ESSAY TIMING

When writing a timed essay, you will spend most of your time writing. But you must also leave time at the beginning for planning and at the end for revising and editing.

The following times can act as a guide for writing a 30-minute timed essay. You may take longer or shorter for any particular step. But remember any time you take longer for a step, leaves you that much less time for other steps.

- **Planning (5 minutes)**
  Brainstorming some ideas
  Writing a rough outline

- **Writing (20 minutes)**
  Writing an introduction
  Writing some body paragraphs
  Writing a brief conclusion

- **Revising and editing (5 minutes)**
  Checking the content
  Editing for grammar
  Editing for mechanics

Your turn

Write an essay to answer *one* of the questions below. Spend 30 minutes to plan, write, revise, and edit your essay. Good luck!

1 What are the three most important characteristics of a friend? Explain your answers.
2 Air pollution is a serious problem in major cities. Pollution could be reduced if more people used public transportation such as trains and buses instead of private cars. Discuss the obstacles to using public transportation and suggest solutions.
3 Think of an interesting or unusual activity, hobby, or sport that you enjoy. Write an essay to explain why others should try the activity.

C Evaluate your own writing

Think about your timed essay and your experience writing it. Fill in the *Self-Reflection Form*.

SELF-REFLECTION FORM

1 Did you write an outline? Was it helpful in organizing your ideas?

_____

2 How long did you spend reading the question, getting ideas, and writing the outline? Did you spend enough time on these steps?

_____

3 Without looking, write the test question here in your own words. Compare it to the actual test question on page 154. Did you understand and answer the original test question?

_____

4 Do your sentences show good variety? _____

5 Did you use transitions to show the connections between ideas? _____

6 How many minutes did you spend writing your essay? _____

7 Did you have time to revise and edit your work? If so, how many minutes did you spend? _____

8 Did your revisions and edits improve your essay? If so, how? _____

_____

9 How much stress did you experience during your writing? How did you manage it?

_____

10 If you were a teacher, what "grade" (a score from 1 to 5) would you give your essay? Why?

_____

11 What will you do differently the next time you write a timed essay?

_____

12 Any other comments: _____

_____

_____

D Benefit from peer feedback

Exchange essays and books with a partner. Fill out the form below about your partner's essay. Then return the book and discuss your answers.

PEER FEEDBACK FORM

Writer's name: _____   Date: _____

Reviewer's name: _____

1 Did your partner write an outline?

2 Answer these questions about the introduction. Mark each box ✓ or X.
   ☐ Does the thesis statement directly address the test question?
   ☐ Does the introduction prepare you for the rest of the essay?

3 Underline the topic sentence of each body paragraph.

4 In each body paragraph, find two ideas that support the topic sentence. Number them. If you cannot find at least two supporting ideas, write "support?" in the margin.

5 Answer these questions about the conclusion. Mark each box ✓ or X.

   ☐ Does the conclusion restate the thesis statement?
   ☐ Does the conclusion summarize the main points?
   ☐ Does the conclusion include a concluding statement?

6 Is there any evidence of revision in the essay?

7 Look at the overall appearance of the essay. Mark each box ✓ or X.
   ☐ Is the essay neat and legible?
   ☐ Is the essay double-spaced?
   ☐ Are changes clean and understandable?

8 Is there a good variety of sentences in the essay? _____

9 Draw a star (★) in the margin next to your favorite sentences. Choose two or three. Put a question mark (?) next to any sentences that you did not understand.

10 What "grade" would you give this essay (a score of 1 to 5)? _____

11 Any other comments: _____

_____

_____

E Check your progress

After you get your essay back from your instructor, complete the *Progress Check* below.

PROGRESS CHECK

Date: _____

Essay title: _____

Things I did well in this timed essay:

_____

_____

_____

Things I want to work on in my next timed essay:

_____

_____

_____

Article 1

The following article on the vulnerability of citizens' personal information is adapted from an article that first appeared in *Forbes* magazine on Novermber 29, 1999. It was accessed at <http://members.forbes.com/forbes/1999/1129/6413182a.html> on February 25, 2007.

The End of Privacy
Adam L. Penenberg

The phone rang and a stranger sang at the other end of the line: "Happy Birthday to you." That was spooky* – the next day I would turn 37. "Your full name is Adam Landis Penenberg," the caller continued. "Landis?" My mother's maiden name*. Then Daniel Cohn, Web detective, told me the rest of my "base identifiers" – my birth date, address in New York, Social Security number*. Just two days earlier I had issued Cohn a challenge: Starting with my byline*, find as much information about me as you can. "That didn't take long," I said.

"It took about five minutes," Cohn said. "I'll have the rest within a week." And the line went dead.

In all of six days, Dan Cohn and his Web detective agency, Docusearch. com, shattered* every notion I had about privacy in this country. Using only a keyboard and the phone, he was able to uncover the innermost details of my life – whom I call late at night; how much money I have in the bank; my salary and rent. He even got my unlisted phone numbers*, both of them.

For decades, information like this was kept in large mainframe computers that were difficult to access. The move to desktop PCs and local servers in the 1990s distributed these data far and wide. Computers now hold half a billion bank accounts, half a billion credit card accounts, hundreds of millions of mortgages and retirement funds and medical claims, and more. The Web links it all together.

As e-commerce grows, marketers and busybodies* can access more consumer data than ever before. It's far worse than you think. Advances in search techniques and the rise of massive databases leave you vulnerable.* The spread of the Web is the final step. It will make most of the secrets you have more instantly available than ever before, ready to reveal* themselves in a few taps on the keyboard.

You may well ask: What's the big deal? We consumers are as much to blame as marketers for all these loose data. We have willingly given up some privacy in exchange for convenience; it is why we use a credit card to shop, even though it means we receive more junk mail. Why should we care if our personal information isn't so personal anymore?

continued

Well, take this test: Next time you are at a party, tell a stranger your salary, checking account balance, mortgage payment, and Social Security number. If this makes you uneasy, you have your answer.

Data sleuths*, like Dan Cohn of Docusearch, are ready to cash in.* Cohn and a team of researchers work out of the top floor of a dull, five-story office building in Boca Raton, Florida, taking orders from 9 a.m. to 4 p.m. Their Web site is open 24 hours a day, 365 days a year. You click through it and load up an online shopping cart as casually as if you were at Amazon. com. Docusearch's clients include lawyers, insurers, private detectives, and businesses. They spy on celebrities, business rivals, or anyone else, for a small price. They fill up to 100 orders a day on the Web, and expect $1 million in business this year. Cohn's firm will get a client your unlisted telephone number for $49, your Social Security number for $49, and your bank balances for $45. Your driving record goes for $35; tracing* a cell phone number costs $84. Cohn will even tell someone what stocks, bonds, and securities you own (for $209).

The researchers use advance search methods, but Cohn also admits to misrepresenting who he is and what he is after. He says the law lets licensed investigators use such tricks as "pretext calling," or fooling company employees into giving out information about customers over the phone (legal in all but a few states).

That's how Cohn finally pierced* my privacy. First, he plugged my name into the credit bureaus online. In minutes, he had my Social Security number, address, and birth date. Credit agencies are supposed to ensure that their subscribers (retailers, auto dealers, banks, mortgage companies) have a legitimate need to check credit; but Cohn says no one has ever checked up on him.

With this information, Cohn next got access to a Federal Reserve database that told him where I had bank deposits. Then he located my bank account: my account balance, direct deposits from work, withdrawals, ATM visits, check numbers with dates and amounts, and the name of my broker.*

How did Cohn get my bank secrets? Directly from the source. Cohn says he phoned the bank and talked to one of 500 employees who can tap into my data. "Hi, I'm Dan Cohn, a licensed state investigator conducting an investigation of an Adam Penenberg," he told the staffer, knowing the words "licensed" and "state" make it sound like he works for law enforcement.

Then he recited my Social Security, birth date, and address, "and before I could get out anything more he spat out* your account number." Cohn told the helpful worker: "I talked to Penenberg's broker, um, I can't remember his name. . . ."

"Dan Dunn?" the bank employee asked. "Yeah, Dan Dunn," Cohn said. The employee then read Cohn my complete history – balance, deposits, withdrawals, check numbers, and amounts.

It was a similar story with my phone numbers. My long distance carrier* said that a Mr. Penenberg had called to inquire about my most recent bill. A company spokesman explained that whoever made the call "posed as you and had enough information to convince our customer service representative that he was you."

For the most part, Cohn's methods are not illegal. "There is no general law that protects consumers' privacy in the U.S.," says David Banisar, a

Washington lawyer who helped found the Electronic Privacy Information Center (www.epic.org). In Europe, companies classified as "data controllers" can't give out your personal details without your permission, but the U.S. has little protection, he says.

Some small protections are in place: a 1984 act protecting cable TV bills; the 1988 Video Privacy Protection Act, passed after a newspaper published the video rental records of Supreme Court nominee Robert Bork. "It's crazy, but your movie rental history is more protected under the law than your credit history is," says Wade, the author of *Identity Theft: The Cybercrime of the Millennium* (Loompanics Unlimited, 1999).

Originally, Social Security numbers weren't used for identification purposes. But today you are required by law to give an accurate number to a bank or other institution that pays you interest or dividends, so that the Internal Revenue Service can make sure you pay the proper taxes. The bank, in turn, just might trade that number away to a credit bureau – even if you aren't applying for credit. That's how people like Cohn can get into so many databases.

Congress might pass a bill* to outlaw* pretext calling. But more than 100 privacy bills filed in the past two years have gone nowhere.

So for now, you have to protect yourself. If you open a bank account with no credit attached to it, ask the bank to keep your Social Security number from credit bureaus. Make sure your broker can – and will – restrict telephone access to your account. If a business without a legitimate need for your Social Security number asks for it, leave the space blank – or write in an incorrect number.

In the meantime, I'm starting over: I will change all of my bank, utility, and credit-card account numbers and apply for new unlisted phone numbers. That should stop the info-brokers for a while – at least for the next week or two.

spooky: *strange and frightening*
maiden name: *the family name a woman has before she marries*
Social Security number: *a number used to identify legal workers in the United States for official purposes such as taxes and insurance*
byline: *a line at the top of a newspaper or magazine article giving the writer's name*
shattered: *destroyed*
unlisted phone numbers: *phone numbers that are not included in the public list of telephone numbers provided by a telephone company*
busybodies: *(informal) people who are too interested in other people's private business*
vulnerable: *able to be attacked*
reveal: *show*
sleuths: *(old-fashioned or humorous) people whose job is to discover information about crimes and find out who is responsible for them; detectives*
cash in: *(informal) make money*
tracing: *finding*
pierced: *broke through*
broker: *a person who buys and sells foreign money, shares in companies, etc., for other people*
spat out: *quickly said out loud*
long distance carrier: *a phone company that gives you service outside the local area*
pass a bill: *give approval to something, especially by voting, to make it law*
outlaw: *make something illegal or unacceptable*

The following article on the existence of a link between playing video games and exhibiting violent behavior is adapted from an article that first appeared in *Slate* magazine on April 27, 2007. It was accessed at <http://www.slate.com/id/2164065/> on July 15, 2007.

Don't Shoot: Why Video Games Really Are Linked to Violence

Amanda Schaffer

Millions of people play the popular first-person-shooter* video games Counter-Strike, Halo, and Doom and never commit violent crimes. But the question is whether exposure to video-game violence is one risk factor for increased aggression: Is it associated with shifts in attitudes or responses that may predispose* kids to commit violent acts? A large body of evidence suggests that this may be so. The studies have their shortcomings, but taken as a whole, they demonstrate that video games have a potent impact on behavior and learning.

Three kinds of research link violent video games to increased aggression. First, there are studies that look for correlations between exposure to these games and real-world aggression. This work suggests that kids who are more immersed* in violent video games may be more likely to get into physical fights, argue with teachers, or display anger and hostility. Second, there is longitudinal research (measuring behavior over time) that assesses gaming habits and belligerence* in a group of children. One example: A study of 430 third-, fourth-, and fifth-graders, published this year by psychologists Craig Anderson, Douglas Gentile, and Katherine Buckley, found that the kids who played more violent video games "changed over the school year to become more verbally aggressive, more physically aggressive," and less helpful to others.

Finally, experimental studies randomly assign subjects to play a violent or a nonviolent game, and then compare their levels of aggression. In work published in 2000, Anderson and Karen Dill randomly assigned 210 undergraduates to play Wolfenstein 3-D, a first-person-shooter game, or Myst, an adventure game in which players explore mazes and puzzles. Anderson and Dill found that when the students went on to play a second game, the Wolfenstein 3-D players were more likely to behave aggressively toward losing opponents. Given the chance to punish with blasts of noise, they chose to inflict significantly louder and longer blasts than the Myst kids did. Other recent work randomly assigned students to play violent or nonviolent games, and then analyzed differences in brain activation patterns using brain scans, but the research is so far difficult to assess.

Each of these approaches has its flaws*. The first kind of correlational study can never prove that video-game playing causes physical aggression. Maybe aggressive people are simply more likely to play violent games in the first place. Meanwhile, the randomized trials, like Anderson and Dill's, which do imply causation, necessarily depend on lab-based measures of aggression, such as whether subjects blast each other with noise. This is a respected measure, but obviously not the same as seeing whether real people hit or shoot each other. The longitudinal work, like this year's elementary-school study, is a useful middle ground: It shows that playing more-violent video games predicts higher levels of verbal and physical aggression later on. It doesn't matter why the kids started playing violent games or whether they were already more aggressive than their peers*; the point is that a year of game-playing likely contributes to making them more aggressive than they were when they started. If we had only one of the three kinds of studies, the findings wouldn't mean much. But taken together, the body of research suggests a real connection.

The connection between violent games and real violence is also fairly intuitive*. In playing the games, kids are likely to become desensitized to violent, bloody images, which could make them less disturbing and perhaps easier to deal with in real life. The games may also encourage kids (and adults) to rehearse aggressive solutions to conflict, meaning that these thought processes may become more available to them when real-life conflicts arise, Anderson says. Video games also offer immediate feedback and constant small rewards – in the form of points, or access to new levels or weapons. And they tend to tailor* tasks to a player's skill level, starting easy and getting harder. That makes them "phenomenal teachers," says Anderson, though "what they teach very much depends on content."

Critics counter that some kids may "use games to vent anger* or distract themselves from problems," as psychiatry professor Cheryl Olson writes. This can be "functional" rather than unhealthy, depending on the kid's mental state and the extent of his game playing. But other studies suggest that venting anger doesn't reduce later aggressive behavior, so this thesis doesn't have the most solid support.

When video games aren't about violence, their capacity to teach can be a good thing. For patients suffering from arachnophobia*, fear of flying, or post-traumatic stress disorder, therapists are beginning to use virtual realities as a desensitization tool. And despite their reputation that they're a waste of time, video games may also teach visual attention and spatial skills. (Recently, a study showed that having played three or more hours of video games a week was a better predictor of some surgeons' skills than their level of surgical training.) The games also work for conveying information to kids that they will remember. Video games that teach diabetic kids how to take better care of themselves, for instance, were shown to decrease their diabetes-related urgent and emergency visits by 77 percent after six months.

Given all of this, it makes sense to be specific about which games may be linked to harmful effects and which to neutral or good ones. Better research is also needed to understand whether some kids are more vulnerable to video-game violence, and how exposure interacts with other risk factors for aggression like poverty, psychological disorders, and a history of abuse. Meanwhile, how about a game in which kids, psychiatrists, and late-night comics size up all these factors and help save the world?

first-person-shooter video games: *video games in which the player sees the action through the eyes of someone shooting other characters in the game*
predispose: *to make someone more likely to behave in a particular way*
immersed: *completely involved in something*
belligerence: *angry or hostile behavior*
flaws: *problems; weaknesses*
intuitive: *understood without needing proof or arguments*
tailor: *adjust*
vent anger: *give open expression to one's anger*
arachnophobia: *fear of spiders*

The following article on whether homework is beneficial for students first appeared in the newspaper *USA Today* on September 14, 2006. It was accessed at <http://www.alfiekohn.org/teaching/kmbraa.htm> on July 15, 2007.

Kids May Be Right After All: Homework Stinks
Alfie Kohn

With the start of a new school year, students once again are shifting impatiently in their seats, working their way through an endless pile of worksheets.

And that's after they come home.

A new study confirms what kids and parents already know: The "tougher standards" fad that has American education in its grip* has meant more and more homework for younger and younger children.

Several years ago, we learned that the proportion of 6-to-8-year-olds who reported having homework on a given day had climbed from 34 percent in 1981 to 58 percent in 1997, and that the weekly time spent studying more than doubled during the same period.

Last month, professor Sandra Hofferth at the University of Maryland released an update to that study. Now, the proportion of young children who had homework on a specific day jumped to 64 percent, and the amount of time they spent on it climbed by another third. Homework rates for 6-to-8 year-olds are now virtually equivalent* to those for 9-to-12-year-olds. And let's not even talk about the high school workload.

What the research shows about the growing burden of homework is disconcerting*. Equally important, however, is what the research *doesn't* show: namely, that homework is necessary or beneficial. We know all about the stress and exhaustion, the family conflict, and loss of time for other activities. ("Our kids are missing out on their childhoods," one Mom laments.*) But we reassure ourselves that it's all worth it because homework raises achievement, teaches independence and good work habits, and helps them to become more successful learners.

Remarkably, however, the data to support those beliefs just don't exist:

- There is no evidence that homework provides any benefits in elementary school. Even if you regard standardized test results as a useful measure (which I don't), homework isn't even *associated* with higher scores at this age. The only effect that does show up is more negative attitudes on the part of students who get more assignments.

- In high school, some studies do find a correlation* between homework and test scores (or grades), but it's usually fairly small, and it has a tendency to disappear when more sophisticated statistical controls are applied. Moreover, there's no evidence that higher achievement is *due* to the homework even when an association does appear.

- International comparisons offer no reassurance. In describing the results of their analysis of student performance across 50 countries, which was published last year, Pennsylvania State University researchers David Baker and Gerald Letendre said: "Not only did we fail to find any positive relationships," but "the overall correlations between national average student achievement and national averages in [amount of homework assigned] . . . are all *negative*.

- Finally, not a single study has ever supported the claim that homework teaches good work habits or develops positive character traits such as self-discipline and independence. These assumptions could be described as urban myths* except for the fact that they're still taken seriously in suburban and rural areas, too.

In short, the research provides no reason to think that students would be at any sort of disadvantage if they got much less homework – or maybe even none at all. And the accounts I've heard from teachers and schools that have abolished* after-school assignments, yet whose students are succeeding brilliantly (while maintaining their enthusiasm about learning) offer evidence of a different sort.

Yet these schools are in the minority, to say the least. As a rule, homework is assigned not merely* on those occasions when the teacher really believes it might help, but on a regular schedule that's been determined ahead of time. And the homework load is growing fastest for younger children, which is precisely where the supporting evidence isn't just shaky* – it's nonexistent.

It's time for us to stop taking the value, and existence, of homework for granted. Rather than confining ourselves to peripheral questions – "What types of binders should kids have?" "Is *x* minutes enough time for this assignment?" – we should ask what really matters: Is the kind of homework our kids are getting worth doing in any amount? What evidence exists to show that daily homework is necessary for children to become better thinkers or more engaged learners?

And: What if, after spending six or seven hours a day at school, we let them have their afternoons and evenings just to be kids?

fad that has American education in its grip: *popular and influential movement for American education*
virtually equivalent: *almost exactly the same*
disconcerting: *problematic; something that makes someone feel worried or troubled*
laments: *says sadly*
correlation: *connection between two things, often one in which one of them causes or influences the other*
urban myths: *common but untrue stories*
abolished: *ended an activity*
merely: *just*
shaky: *not firm or strong*

Credits